First World War
and Army of Occupation
War Diary
France, Belgium and Germany

21 DIVISION
62 Infantry Brigade
Alexandra, Princess of Wales's Own (Yorkshire Regiment)
10th Battalion
1 January 1915 - 27 February 1918

WO95/2156/2

The Naval & Military Press Ltd
www.nmarchive.com
Published in association with The National Archives

Published by

The Naval & Military Press Ltd

Unit 10 Ridgewood Industrial Park,

Uckfield, East Sussex,

TN22 5QE England

Tel: +44 (0) 1825 749494

www.naval-military-press.com

www.nmarchive.com

This diary has been reprinted in facsimile from the original. Any imperfections are inevitably reproduced and the quality may fall short of modern type and cartographic standards.

© Crown Copyright
Images reproduced by permission of The National Archives, London, England, 2015.

Contents

Document type	Place/Title	Date From	Date To
Heading	WO95/2156-2		
Heading	10th Bn Yorkshire Regt Sep 1915-Feb 1918		
Heading	10th Battn. The Yorkshire Regiment. September (9.9.15-30.9.15) 1915		
War Diary	Whitley	09/09/1915	09/09/1915
War Diary	Boulogne	10/09/1915	10/09/1915
War Diary	Pont-De-Briques.	11/09/1915	11/09/1915
War Diary	Houlle	20/09/1915	20/09/1915
War Diary	Wittes	21/09/1915	21/09/1915
War Diary	Ames	22/09/1915	22/09/1915
War Diary	Bur Bure	24/09/1915	24/09/1915
War Diary	Noeux-Le-Mines	25/09/1915	25/09/1915
War Diary	Vermelles	26/09/1915	26/09/1915
War Diary	Loos	27/09/1915	27/09/1915
War Diary	Bivouac Near Philosophe	28/09/1915	28/09/1915
War Diary	Burgette	29/09/1915	29/09/1915
Heading	21st Division 10th Yorkshire Regt. Vol: 2 Oct 15		
War Diary	Quernes	01/10/1915	01/10/1915
War Diary	Morbecque	02/10/1915	02/10/1915
War Diary	Strazeele	03/10/1915	13/10/1915
War Diary	Merris	14/10/1915	14/10/1915
War Diary	Armentieres	15/10/1915	31/10/1915
Heading	21st Division Nov 15		
War Diary	Armentieres	01/11/1915	30/11/1915
Heading	21st Division 10th Yorkshire Vol 4 December 1915		
War Diary	Armentieres	01/12/1915	06/12/1915
War Diary	Trenches	07/12/1915	09/12/1915
War Diary	Armentieres	10/12/1915	15/12/1915
War Diary	Trenches	16/12/1915	21/12/1915
War Diary	Armentieres	22/12/1915	31/12/1915
Heading	10th Yorks Regt Vol 6 21st Div		
Heading	10th Yorks Vol 5		
War Diary	Armentieres	01/01/1915	29/02/1915
Heading	10 York Reg Vol 7		
War Diary	Armentieres	01/03/1916	02/03/1916
War Diary	Houplines	03/03/1916	08/03/1916
War Diary	Armentieres	09/03/1916	22/03/1916
War Diary	Sternwercke	23/03/1916	31/03/1916
War Diary	Field	02/04/1916	30/04/1916
War Diary	Meaulte	01/05/1916	02/05/1916
War Diary	Ville	03/05/1916	03/05/1916
War Diary	Laneuville	04/05/1916	12/05/1916
War Diary	K.18.d.8.6	13/05/1916	22/05/1916
War Diary	Meaulte	23/05/1916	27/05/1916
War Diary	Trenches	28/05/1916	01/06/1916
War Diary	Buire	02/06/1916	02/06/1916
War Diary	Laneuville	03/06/1916	11/06/1916
War Diary	Meaulte	12/06/1916	20/06/1916
War Diary	Redoubts Becordel	21/06/1916	24/06/1916
War Diary	Redoubts Etc.	25/06/1916	27/06/1916

War Diary	Queens Road	28/06/1916	28/06/1916
War Diary	Buire	29/06/1916	30/06/1916
Heading	10th Battn. The Yorkshire Regiment. July 1916		
War Diary	In The Field	01/07/1916	03/07/1916
War Diary	Dernancourt	04/07/1916	04/07/1916
War Diary	Ailly S. Somme	05/07/1916	07/07/1916
War Diary	Moulliens Vidame	08/07/1916	10/07/1916
War Diary	Meaulte	11/07/1916	11/07/1916
War Diary	In The Field	12/07/1916	12/07/1916
War Diary	Mametz Wood	13/07/1916	17/07/1916
War Diary	Buire	18/07/1916	20/07/1916
War Diary	Moulliens Wd	21/07/1916	22/07/1916
War Diary	Rifle Range	23/07/1916	23/07/1916
War Diary	Ternas	24/07/1916	24/07/1916
War Diary	Manin	25/07/1916	27/07/1916
War Diary	Arras	28/07/1917	28/07/1917
War Diary	Trenches	29/07/1916	31/07/1916
Heading	1/10th Battalion Yorkshire Regiment August 1916.		
War Diary	Trenches	01/08/1916	03/08/1916
War Diary	Agnes-Les-Duisans	04/08/1916	09/08/1916
War Diary	Trenches	10/08/1916	18/08/1916
War Diary	Arras	19/08/1916	26/08/1916
War Diary	Trenches	27/08/1916	31/08/1916
Heading	1/10th Battalion Yorkshire Regiment September 1916		
War Diary	In Trenches	01/09/1916	01/09/1916
War Diary	Daneville	02/09/1916	02/09/1916
War Diary	Somberin	03/09/1916	12/09/1916
War Diary	Rebreuviette	13/09/1916	13/09/1916
War Diary	Bivouac	14/09/1916	16/09/1916
War Diary	Trenches	17/09/1916	22/09/1916
War Diary	Bivouac	23/09/1916	26/09/1916
War Diary	Trenches	27/09/1916	29/09/1916
War Diary	Bivouac	30/09/1916	30/09/1916
War Diary	In The Field	01/10/1916	01/10/1916
War Diary	Buire	02/10/1916	03/10/1916
War Diary	Villiers Sur. Ailly	04/10/1916	08/10/1916
War Diary	Marles Lez Mines	09/10/1916	10/10/1916
War Diary	Fouquereuil	11/10/1916	11/10/1916
War Diary	Trenches	12/10/1916	27/12/1916
War Diary	Houchin	28/12/1916	28/12/1916
War Diary	Marles	29/12/1916	31/12/1916
War Diary	Marles Les-Mines (Hazebrouke 5A)	01/01/1917	09/01/1917
War Diary	Marles Les-Mines	09/01/1917	27/01/1917
War Diary	Peselhoek	28/01/1917	31/01/1917
Miscellaneous			
War Diary	Field	01/02/1917	28/02/1917
Miscellaneous	Move Orders 26. 10th Bn. Yorkshire Regiment.	28/02/1917	28/02/1917
War Diary	Field	01/03/1917	31/03/1917
Miscellaneous	Move Orders 26A 10th Bn. Yorkshire Regiment.	02/03/1917	02/03/1917
Miscellaneous	Move Orders 27 10th Bn. Yorkshire Regiment.	08/03/1917	08/03/1917
Miscellaneous	Move Orders 30 10th Bn. Yorkshire Regiment.	10/03/1917	10/03/1917
Miscellaneous	Move Orders 31 10th Bn. Yorkshire Regiment.		
Miscellaneous	Move Orders No 31A 10th Bn Yorkshire Regiment.	12/03/1917	12/03/1917
Miscellaneous	Move Orders No 32 10th Bn. Yorkshire Regiment.	25/03/1917	25/03/1917
Operation(al) Order(s)	Operation Order No 33 10th Bn. Yorkshire Regiment.	26/03/1917	26/03/1917
Miscellaneous	O.C. "A" Coy B.O.	27/03/1917	27/03/1917

Operation(al) Order(s)	Operation Orders No. 34 10th Bn. Yorkshire Regiment	27/03/1917	27/03/1917
Operation(al) Order(s)	Operation Order No. 35 10th Bn. Yorkshire Regiment	20/03/1917	20/03/1917
War Diary	In The Field	01/04/1917	05/04/1917
War Diary	Adinfer	06/04/1917	08/04/1917
War Diary	In The Field	09/04/1917	11/04/1917
War Diary	Boiry Becquerelle	12/04/1917	15/04/1917
War Diary	Beaumetz	16/04/1917	24/04/1917
War Diary	Mercatel	25/04/1917	26/04/1917
War Diary	Boiry Becquerelle	27/04/1917	29/04/1917
War Diary	In The Field	30/04/1917	12/05/1917
War Diary	Hendecourt	13/05/1917	31/05/1917
War Diary	Field	01/06/1917	10/10/1917
War Diary	Billets	10/10/1917	20/10/1917
War Diary	Billets Sercus	10/10/1917	20/10/1917
War Diary	Field	20/10/1917	31/10/1917
Heading	10th Yorkshire Regt November 1917		
War Diary	Ypres Area	01/11/1917	30/11/1917
Operation(al) Order(s)	19th South York Regt. Order No. 19	02/11/1917	02/11/1917
Map	Message Map.		
Operation(al) Order(s)	10th Yorkshire Regiment. Order No. 80	03/11/1917	03/11/1917
Map	Message Map		
Operation(al) Order(s)	10th Yorkshire Regiment. Order No. 81	07/11/1917	07/11/1917
Miscellaneous	Amendment to 10th Yorkshire Order No. 81		
Miscellaneous	10th Yorkshire Regiment Defence Scheme Support Battalion	09/11/1917	09/11/1917
Miscellaneous	62nd Infantry Brigade Defence Scheme.	08/11/1917	08/11/1917
Miscellaneous	Appendix "A" Position of Machine Guns		
Miscellaneous	Appendix "B" Communications		
Operation(al) Order(s)	10th Yorkshire Regiment Order No. 82	10/11/1917	10/11/1917
Miscellaneous	Casualties-4th to 11th November 1917		
Operation(al) Order(s)	10th Bn. Yorkshire Regt Order No. 83	13/11/1917	13/11/1917
Miscellaneous	10th Yorkshire Regt. Addition to Order 84	10/11/1917	10/11/1917
Operation(al) Order(s)	10th Yorkshire Regt Order No 84	15/11/1917	15/11/1917
Operation(al) Order(s)	10th Yorkshire Regiment Order No. 85	17/11/1917	17/11/1917
Operation(al) Order(s)	10th Bn. Yorkshire Regt Order No. 86	18/11/1917	18/11/1917
Miscellaneous	10th Bn. Yorkshire Regt Addition to Order 86	18/11/1917	18/11/1917
Operation(al) Order(s)	10th Yorkshire Regt Order No. 87	19/11/1917	19/11/1917
Operation(al) Order(s)	10 Yorkshire Regt. Order No. 88	20/11/1917	20/11/1917
Operation(al) Order(s)	10 Yorkshire Regt. Order No. A2	23/11/1917	23/11/1917
Miscellaneous	10th Yorkshire Regt. Addition Order A2	24/11/1917	24/11/1917
Operation(al) Order(s)	10th York Regt. Order No. 2	30/11/1917	30/11/1917
Heading	10 Bn Yorkshire Regt. for month of Dec 1917		
War Diary	Brusle	01/12/1917	03/12/1917
War Diary	Longavesnes	04/12/1917	07/12/1917
War Diary	Heudicourt	07/12/1917	12/12/1917
War Diary	Trenches	13/12/1917	14/12/1917
War Diary	Rly Embankment (to.23.b.)	15/12/1917	17/12/1917
War Diary	Longavesnes	18/12/1917	28/12/1917
War Diary	Trenches	29/12/1917	31/12/1917
Operation(al) Order(s)	10th Yorkshire Regiment Order No. 3	03/12/1917	03/12/1917
Operation(al) Order(s)	10 Yorkshire Regt. Order No 4	06/12/1917	06/12/1917
Operation(al) Order(s)	10 Yorkshire Regt. Order No 5	08/12/1917	08/12/1917
Operation(al) Order(s)	10th Yorkshire Regiment. Order No. 6	13/12/1917	13/12/1917
Miscellaneous			
Operation(al) Order(s)	10th Yorkshire Regiment. Order No. 8	16/12/1917	16/12/1917
Operation(al) Order(s)	10th Yorkshire Regiment. Order No. 10		

War Diary	Field	01/01/1918	27/02/1918
Miscellaneous	Addition To 10th Yorkshire Regt. Order No. 20		
Operation(al) Order(s)	10th Yorkshire Regiment Order No. 31	19/01/1917	19/01/1917
Operation(al) Order(s)	10th Yorkshire Regiment. Order No. 15	11/01/1918	11/01/1918
Operation(al) Order(s)	10th Yorkshire Regiment. Order No. 15A	18/01/1918	18/01/1918
Operation(al) Order(s)	10th Yorkshire Regiment. Order No. 16	19/01/1918	19/01/1918
Operation(al) Order(s)	10th Yorkshire Regiment. Order No. 17		
Operation(al) Order(s)	10 Yorkshire Regiment. Order No. 18		
Operation(al) Order(s)	10th Yorkshire Regiment. Order No. 19		
Operation(al) Order(s)	10th Yorkshire Regiment. Order No. 20	29/01/1918	29/01/1918

13095215b12

21ST DIVISION
62ND INFY BDE

10TH BN YORKSHIRE REGT
SEP 1915 - FEB 1918

DISBANDED

62nd Inf.Bde.
21st Div.

Battn. disembarked
Boulogne from
England 10.9.15.

10th BATTN. THE YORKSHIRE REGIMENT.

S E P T E M B E R
(9.9.15-30.9.15)

1 9 1 5

Army Form C. 2118

Sheet. No. 1.

WAR DIARY
or
INTELLIGENCE SUMMARY
(Erase heading not required.)

Instructions regarding War Diaries and Intelligence Summaries are contained in F.S. Regs., Part II. and the Staff Manual respectively. Title Pages will be prepared in manuscript.

Place	Date 1915	Hour	Summary of Events and Information	Remarks and references to Appendices
Whitley	Sept. 9th	6.P.M.	Left Whitley Camp and marched to MILFORD. entrained here for FOLKESTON. arrived there about 11.40 p.m. and embarked at once.	I.J.
BOULOGNE	10th	3.15 A.M.	Arrived BOULOGNE after a good crossing. No incidents on the way. Went into rest camp.	I.J.
PONT-DE-BRIQUES.	11th	3.A.M.	Entrained at this place travelled through the night. and detrained at WATTEN. about 9.40 A.M. breakfast. and then marched to HOULLE. into Billets. Stayed there till. 20th.	I.J.
HOULLE	20th	6.20 P.M.	Left HOULLE and marched through night to WITTES. into Bivouac.	I.J.
WITTES.	21st	6. P.M.	Left WITTES. do	I.J.
AMES.	22nd	6. P.M.	do AMES. to AMES. do	I.J.
			to BUR.BURE. went into Billets for two nights	I.J.
			had heavy rain & thunder.	
BUR.BURE.	24th	6.30 P.M.	Left BUR.BURE. in evening and marched to NOEUX-LE-MINES. arrived there early	I.J.
			in the morning. about 1 A.M. and Bivouaced.	
NOEUX-LE-MINES.	25th	abt 11 a.m.	Moved from NOEUX-LE-MINES. to VERMELLES.	I.J.

Army Form C. 2118

Sheet No 2.

WAR DIARY
or
INTELLIGENCE SUMMARY
(Erase heading not required.)

Instructions regarding War Diaries and Intelligence Summaries are contained in F. S. Regs., Part II. and the Staff Manual respectively. Title Pages will be prepared in manuscript.

Place	Date	Hour	Summary of Events and Information	Remarks and references to Appendices
VERMELLES.	Sept. 26th	3.15. p.m.	Moved from VERMELLES to attack HILL 70. through village of LOOS. Attacked about 3.45.p.m. The Battn attacked, and reached the first line of fire trenches and supported the 18th LONDON. REGT. The Battn lost heavily. A.C.D & half B. Coy. were on right of SLAG. HEAP. road of CHALK. PIT. on night of 18th. LONDON. REGT. near LOOS. PYLONS. remainder of B. Coy. & remaining B. Coys were moved to left of SLAG. HEAP and during night of 26th & 27th A.C.D. & half B. Coys waited during the night to attack again.	1.f
LOOS.	27.	9.A.M.	Attack on HILL 70. re-commenced. This attack went on all day with very (Col. HADOW) little success, the Battn again lost heavily, including the Colonel and 2nd in Command (Maj. DENT) and 11 other officers killed and wounded. The order to retire was given, and the Battn returned to Bivouac about midnight near PHILOSOPHE. B. Coy got orders to retire about 10 A.M. on the 28th from night of CHALK. PIT. and got into Bivouac about 3. p.m. Major Eddowes was appointed to Command the Regiment.	1.f
BIVOUAC. near PHILOSOPHE.	28	5.20 p.m.	Moved from Bivouac. to NOEUX-LE-MINES. and entrained about 1 A.M. the 29th	1.f

Army Form C. 2118.

WAR DIARY
or
INTELLIGENCE SUMMARY.
(Erase heading not required.)

Instructions regarding War Diaries and Intelligence Summaries are contained in F. S. Regs., Part II. and the Staff Manual respectively. Title pages will be prepared in manuscript.

Place	Date	Hour	Summary of Events and Information	Remarks and references to Appendices

---

Army Form C. 2118

Sheet No 3.

WAR DIARY
or
INTELLIGENCE SUMMARY
(Erase heading not required.)

Instructions regarding War Diaries and Intelligence Summaries are contained in F. S. Regs., Part II. and the Staff Manual respectively. Title Pages will be prepared in manuscript.

Place	Date	Hour	Summary of Events and Information	Remarks and references to Appendices
BURGETTE.	Sept 29.	2 A.M.	Detrained at BURGETTE (a fearfully wet night) went into Billets and stayed there till Oct 1st	6.45 AM 1/7.

21st Known

121/7595

10th Yorkshire Rgt.
Vol. 2
Oct 15

2. B.
7 whole

Army Form C. 2118.

WAR DIARY
or
INTELLIGENCE SUMMARY.

10/Yorkshire Rgt.

(Erase heading not required.)

Title pages October 1915

Place	Date	Hour	Summary of Events and Information	Remarks and references to Appendices
QUERNES.	Oct. 1st	6.15 AM	Marched from QUERNES to MORBEQUE. arrived there at 12.30 pm. and went into Billets for the night.	V.T.
MORBEQUE	2nd	8.40 AM	Marched from MORBEQUE through HAZEBROUCK to STRAZEELE. arrived there at 11.30 a.m. and went into Billets.	V.T.
STRAZEELE	3rd	—	In Billets at STRAZEELE. ordinary Coy. & Battn. work & routine.	V.T.
do.	4th	—	do.	Inspection by Brigadier General WILKINSON. V.T.

W.R. Addwes
Major
Commdg. 10. Bn. Yorkshire Regt.

1/10th Yorkshire Regt.

Army Form C. 2118

Sheet 1.

WAR DIARY
or
INTELLIGENCE SUMMARY
(Erase heading not required.)

Place	Date	Hour	Summary of Events and Information	Remarks and references to Appendices
STRAZEELE.	Oct. 5.		In billets at STRAZEELE had a rout march. Coy and Battn work.	V.T.
do.	6.		Do. Company work.	V.T.
do.	7.		Do.	V.T.
do.	8.		Do. Inspection by Major General FORRESTIER-WALKER.	V.T.
do.	9.		Do. Eleven Officers arrived from Base. posted to Coys as follows. A. Coy. Lieut COLLIER. 2.Lt. JARDINE. 2.Lt. T.R.EVANS. B. Coy. 2.Lt. H.SUCH. 2.Lt. BASS. C. Coy. 2.Lt. B.M.CUST. 2.Lt. G.M.LAWLESS. 2.Lt. W.M.SLATER. D. Coy. 2.Lt. F.O.PARKER. 2.Lt. O.H.BALL. 2.Lt. A.R.SLATER.	V.T.
do.	10.		Do. Company work and refitting.	V.T.
do.	11.		Do. received a draft of 200 men from Base. and 25 absentees. who did not arrive at WITLEY in time to come abroad with the Battn.	V.T.
do.	12.		Do. Company work & rout march.	V.T.
do.	13.		Left STRAZEELE at 2.45 p.m. and marched to MERRIS arrived there about 4. p.m. and went into billets for the night.	V.T.
MERRIS.	14.		Left MERRIS at 12.30 p.m. marched through LEVERRIER.— STEENWERCK.— LA.MENEGATE. HALTE.— NIEPPE.— PONT. DE. NIEPPE.—. ARMENTIERES. arrived there about 5.30 p.m. and Battn went into billets	V.T.

10 Yorkshire Regt.

Army Form C. 2118

WAR DIARY
or
INTELLIGENCE SUMMARY
(Erase heading not required.)

Sheet 2

Place	Date	Hour	Summary of Events and Information	Remarks and references to Appendices
ARMENTIERES.	Oct. 15.		In Billets at ARMENTIERES some Officers and N.C.O's went into the trenches for 24 hrs to be instructed in trench warfare and duties.	1.7.
do.	16.		In Billets at ARMENTIERES. some Officers and N.C.O's went into the trenches for 24 hrs to be instructed in trench warfare and duties. Four platoons and officers who went into trenches on 15th went into trenches to take up duties for 24 hours. Sgt. WOOTTON. (D.Coy) wounded on 15th. L. Cpl. SINTON. (D.Coy) do.	1.7.
do.	17.		Do. two platoons of each Company and officers went into trenches for instructions for 24 hours. 2.Lt. W.M.SLATER. wounded. No. 18992. Pte. G. HEPPELL. Killed on 14th. No. 12077 (Act) L.Cpl. A.DEVANEY. wounded... 16th. No. 14124 (Act) L.Cpl. J. RAMSEY. do. 17th. No. 19641 L.Cpl. W. HOCKING. do. 17th.	1.7.
do.	18.		Do. Company went in a new draft of men expected on 19th.	1.7.
do.	19.		Do. Two Companies went into the trenches to relieve two Coys of other Regiments for 24 hours (A.T.C. Coy instructional purpose) A draft of 100 men & N.C.O's arrived. Col. STUBBS. (A Coy) was granted the D.C.M. for meritorious conduct at Loos.	1.7.

Army Form C. 2118

Sheet 3.

10 Yorkshire Regt.

WAR DIARY
or
INTELLIGENCE SUMMARY
(Erase heading not required.)

Place	Date	Hour	Summary of Events and Information	Remarks and references to Appendices
ARMENTIERES.	Oct 20.		In Billets at ARMENTIERES. Two Coys went into the trenches (B & D) to relieve two Coys of the Regt. for 48 hours (instructional purposes) No 17345 Pte W. H. ARTHUR wounded. (D Coy) No 17396 Pte J. T. DODDS. do (D Coy).	I.f.
do.	21.		B & D Coys still in trenches. Other two Coys doing Company work and route march. No 12853 Pte G. H. WORTHY wounded. (B Coy). No 20396 Pte L. McKENNA. do. (B Coy).	I.f.
do.	22.		Companies out of trenches. Company work and route march.	I.f.
do.	23.		Company work and route march. a draft of 20 men NCOs arrived.	I.f.
do.	24.		do.	I.f.
do.	25.		The Battn went into trenches. paraded at 5 p.m. relieving. 5th BORDER REGT. 7th NORTHUMBERLAND FUSILIERS. and 8th DURHAM L.INF. relief completed at 9.30 p.m.	I.f.
do.	26.		In trenches. 78.79.80. No 19210 Pte. S.T. HILL shot himself in the arm. Three platoons of the 8th E. Yorks. Regt. came to the trenches for instruction.	I.f.

WAR DIARY or **INTELLIGENCE SUMMARY**

Army Form C. 2118
Sheet 4.

10 Yorkshire Regt.

Place	Date	Hour	Summary of Events and Information	Remarks and references to Appendices
ARMENTIERES	Oct 24.		In trenches 78.79.80. Inspection by Brigadier General CLIFFORD. A Party of one officer and thirty men left the trenches on the night of the 26th for the purpose of being inspected at BAILLEU by His Majesty King GEORGE V. Nothing of particular interest reported from 6 A.M. on the 26th to 6 A.M. on the 27th. Four Officers and three platoons (new) of the 8th E. YORKS. REGT came to the trenches for instruction.	I.T.
do.	28.		In trenches 78.79.80. Inspection by 2nd Corps Commander Genl. Sir CHARLES FERGUSSON. at 10.30 A.M. who inspected the whole of the fire trench from 60.79.78. No. 2n923 Pte. J.H. STOREY. (A Coy) shot himself in the hand. nothing of particular interest reported between 6 A.M. on 27th and 6 A.M. the 28th.	I.T.
do.	29.		In trenches 78.79.80. The wet weather is causing much trouble in the front line fire trench, and constant falls take place. No. 14124 Pte. L. Cpl. T. Ramsey reported wounded on the 14th now reported "Died of Wounds". Nothing special reported between 6 am on 28th and 6 am on 29th --	I.T.
do.	30.		In trenches 78.79.80. a lot of rebuilding of parapets necessary. it seems rotten in many places. Trench 80. was partly flooded by the overflowing of a ditch. but was soon put straight again at 6 pm on 29th. Our Artillery and M. Guns had a 5 min. bombardment of a suspected German dump. and again at 6.30 pm. it seemed to be successful in keeping the Germans quiet. With the exception of the above nothing important happened between 6 AM on the 29th and 6 AM on the 30th.	I.T.

Army Form C. 2118

10 Yorks. Regt.

Sheet 5.

WAR DIARY
or
INTELLIGENCE SUMMARY
(Erase heading not required.)

Instructions regarding War Diaries and Intelligence Summaries are contained in F. S. Regs., Part II. and the Staff Manual respectively. Title Pages will be prepared in manuscript.

Place	Date	Hour	Summary of Events and Information	Remarks and references to Appendices
ARMENTIERES	Oct. 31.		In trenches 78. 79. 80. The usual repair work and patrol work at night. Nothing of importance reported between 6 A.M. Oct. 30th. and 6 A.M. Oct. 31st. No. 19521 Pte. ALTON. J.G. (A Coy) was wounded on Oct. 30th.	17.

1875 Wt. W593/826 1,000,000 4/15 J.B.C. & A. A.D.S.S./Forms/C. 2118.

21st K Wraun

1st E Yorkshire
Vol. 3

12/
7624

Nov 15

S. B.
8 shots

Army Form C. 2118

10 Yorkshire Regt.

Instructions regarding War Diaries and Intelligence Summaries are contained in F.S. Regs., Part II. and the Staff Manual respectively. Title Pages will be prepared in manuscript.

WAR DIARY
or
INTELLIGENCE SUMMARY
(Erase heading not required.)

Sheet No. 1.

Place	Date	Hour	Summary of Events and Information	Remarks and references to Appendices
ARMENTIÈRES	Nov. 1.	—	In trenches 78. 79. 80 many falls of parapets and traverses, which have to be repaired at once. nothing important reported between 6am on 31st Oct and 6am Nov.1.	
do.	2.	—	In trenches 78. 79. 80 very wet weather and numerous falls of earth in fire trenches and communication trenches. nothing important reported between 6am Nov.1. and 6am Nov 2. No. 17325 Private M. POTTS. (D Coy) wounded Nov. 1. The Battn. was relieved by the 12th and 13th NORTHUMBERLAND FUSRS. The relief commencing at 5.45 pm. and was completed at 9.30 pm. and the Battn. went into billets in ARMENTIÈRES. A & D Coy in BRIGADE.RESERVE. B & C Coys in DIVISIONAL Do. & Billets in ARMENTIÈRES.	
do	3.		Battn. Coys cleaning up and bathing. Lieut. & Adjt. HOLLINGSWORTH appointed temporary Staff Capt. on 62nd BRIGADE Staff.	
do.	4.		do. Several working parties went up to trenches to help in repairs and retrieving work. The remaining Coys doing Coy work, road mending and bathing.	
do.	5.		do. Working parties sent to trenches for repair work etc. No. 17294 Private J. E. BERTHRAM. (C Coy) wounded. 14331 do. J. J. SHEPHERD. (C Coy) do. 14342 do. G. WILSON. (C Coy) do.	
do.	6.		do. bathing parades and resting. The Battn. paraded at 5.30 pm. in order to take over trenches 74. 75. 76. 77. and relieve the 8th E. YORKS. Regt. The relief of trenches was completed by 9. pm.	

10 Yorkshire Regt.

Army Form C. 2118

WAR DIARY
or
INTELLIGENCE SUMMARY
(Erase heading not required.)

Sheet No 2.

Place	Date	Hour	Summary of Events and Information	Remarks and references to Appendices
ARMENTIERES.	Jan. 7.	—	In trenches 74.75.76.77. Trenches in a very bad state. All working parties concentrated on fire trench parapets and traverses. Several dug-outs fell in during the night, nothing reported between 9 p.m. on 6 Jany. and 6 a.m. on 7 Jany. 2nd Lieut. T.R.EVANS. (A Coy) wounded about 8 a.m. on 7th.	

do.	8.	—	In trenches 74.75.76.77. A good deal of Artillery fire on both sides; men busy re-building parapets & other work.
			 No. 17968 Private J.BELL. (D. Coy) Killed.
			     14954 do. T.F.JONES. (H. Coy) do.
			     15949 do. C.F.JOHNSON. (C. Coy) wounded.
			     17343 do. T.WISEMAN. (C Coy) do.
			     20398 do. J.APPS. (A Coy) do.	

do.	9.	—	do. Men working on rebuilding parapets and general repair work. 2nd Lieut. B.M.CUST. (C. Coy) accidentally killed. He was buried about 4.30 p.m. near the Cemetery. ARMENTIERES. Brigadier General had BINNING commanding 62nd Inf. Bgd. was present also. MAJOR. EDDOWES. (C/o York Regt.) and other officers.	
do.	10.	—	do. Working on repair of trenches. Nothing important to report. No. 25040 Private F.FORD. (D Co) Killed. 16431 do. R.TAITE. (C Coy) wounded.	

do.	11.	—	do. Weather quite fine & a good dry up wind, men able to get on much better with repairs. Here very few statists worked with, very little shell fire, and a good deal of aeroplane work has been done.
			 No. 18884 Private R.BYERS. (A Coy) wounded.
			     13724 do. C.W.BELL. (A Coy) do.
			     15818 do. J.TATTERS. (A Coy) do.
			     F628 A/Cpl. M.E.TWIST. (A Coy) do.	

1/6 Yorkshire Regt.

Army Form C. 2118

WAR DIARY
or
INTELLIGENCE SUMMARY
(Erase heading not required.)

Sheet No 3.

Instructions regarding War Diaries and Intelligence Summaries are contained in F.S. Regs., Part II. and the Staff Manual respectively. Title Pages will be prepared in manuscript.

Place	Date	Hour	Summary of Events and Information	Remarks and references to Appendices
ARMENTIERES	Nov. 12	—	In trenches 74, 75, 76, 77. Weather turned wet again & bad night. Some falling in of front line trench. Communication trenches/bordes. No 13438 Private H. RUMNEY. (A Coy) wounded. 11244 L/Cpl. T. STIFF. (B Coy) do. 18124 L/Cpl. J.S. TWIGG. (D Coy) do. 12641 Pvt. R.H. LEACH. (A Coy) do.	
do.	13.	—	do. a very wet night. Work done on parapets, traverses etc. No 14291 Private P. RYAN (A Coy) wounded.	
do.	14.	—	do. had a fine day, and able to get on well with work. Nothing reported between 6 a.m. on Nov. 13 and 6 a.m. on Nov. 14. No 14494 Private A. MITCHELL (D Coy) Killed. 19414 Cch. Cpl. E. IRWIN. (B Coy) wounded 19431 Pvt. J. HOY. (C Coy) do.	
do.	15.	—	do. Good work done in retrenching. The Battn were relieved by the 1st LINCOLN. Regt. and went into Billets in ARMENTIERES. The relief commenced at 5.30 p.m. and was completed at 8.15 p.m.	
do.	16.	—	In Billets at ARMENTIERES the Battn cleaning kit etc. and bathing.	
do.	17.	—	do. Coy work and route marches. a heavy fire of Enemy Artillery about 2.30 to 3.30 a.m. into the town. Not much damage	
do.	18.	—	do. Coy work and route marches. a heavy bombardment of the town by the Enemy. For about one & a half hours a great deal of damage done. No casualties in the Battn.	

10 Yorkshire Regt

Army Form C. 2118

WAR DIARY
or
INTELLIGENCE SUMMARY
(Erase heading not required.)

Sheet No. 4.

Place	Date	Hour	Summary of Events and Information	Remarks and references to Appendices
ARMENTIERES	Jan. 19.	—	In Billets at ARMENTIERES. Coy. work. a very quiet day.	
do.	20.	—	do. Coy. work. a quiet day.	
			No. 14242 Act. L/Cpl. A.E. PALMER. (A Coy) wounded.	
			20393 Pvt. R. HURST. (C Coy) do	
do.	21.	—	do. no parade.	
			The Battn. went into trenches 74.75.76.77. to relieve the Battn.	
			doing duty. (1st LINCOLN Regt). The relief commenced at 6 p.m. & was completed at 9.15 p.m.	
do.	22.	—	In trenches 74.75.76.77. Work on parapets etc. continued under the ROYAL ENGINEERS.	
			Communication trench clearing commenced.	
do.	23.	—	do. No. 9429. Cpl. H. COLLIER. (D Coy) wounded.	
			Repairs work going forward.	
			No. 20282 Private J. WILSON. (B. Coy) Killed.	
			13163 do C. HARRISON. (A. Coy) wounded.	
			15513 do J. CONLEY. (C. Coy) do	
			14390 do C.R.A. DUTTON. (D Coy) Killed.	
			14353 do T. BARLOW. (D Coy) wounded.	
			13726 Cpl. J. GOODWIN. (A Coy) do	
			14290 Private. T. SIMPSON. (A Coy) do	
do.	24.	—	do. Thaw set in with rain. trenches rather wet and some falling	
			in of parapets. work of re-building going on satisfactorily.	
			2nd Lieut W.W. BALL. (B. Coy) Killed about 6.30 am. was turning about	
			6.30 p.m. man Cemetery at ARMENTIERES. Several officers attended funeral.	

1875 Wt. W593/826 1,000,000 4/15 J.B.C. & A. A.D.S.S./Forms/C. 2118.

10 Yorkshire Regt.

WAR DIARY or INTELLIGENCE SUMMARY

Army Form C. 2118

Sheet No 5.

Place	Date	Hour	Summary of Events and Information	Remarks and references to Appendices
ARMENTIERES.	Jan. 25.	—	In trenches 74. 75. 76. 77. Another wet day and water collecting in trenches in spite of pumping. Nothing important reported. No. 15830. Private J. DODDS. (D Coy) wounded.	
do.	26.	—	do. A very quiet night, very wet, we had frost and snow during the night. Patrols were out in front of all trenches and nothing important was reported up to 6 A.M.	
do.	27.	—	do. Repair work under R.E. going on well. A cold fine day. The Battn. were relieved by the 1st LINCOLN Regt. and went into billets at ARMENTIERES. The relief was commenced at 6 P.M. and was completed at 8.45 P.M. No. 14525 Private W. SWAINSTON. (D Coy). wounded. 17418 do. G. GIBSON. (D Coy) do. 7958 do. T. SORRELL. (B Coy) do. D. Coy in Subsidiary trenches for the night.	
do.	28.	—	In Billets at ARMENTIERES. Battn. cleaning clothing and equipment. A. Coy in Subsidiary trenches for the night.	
do.	29.	—	In Billets at ARMENTIERES. Battn. Bathing inspection at 2.30 P.M. a very quiet day. A working party of 200 men provided. B. Coy in Subsidiary trenches for the night.	

10 Yorkshire Regt.

Army Form C. 2118

WAR DIARY or INTELLIGENCE SUMMARY

Sheet No. 6.

Place	Date	Hour	Summary of Events and Information	Remarks and references to Appendices
ARMENTIERES	Nov 30.	—	In Billets at ARMENTIERES. rather heavy bombardment by Germans during the night. The Battn. had no casualties. Bywork etc. A working party of 200 men were provided for 1st LINCOLN Regt. No. 12921 Private T. CAREY. (C.Coy.) killed. 10341 Act. L/Cpl. E. HAGGER (C.Coy.) wounded. 22884 Private F. GODWIN. (C.Coy.) do. 9048 do. W. COX. (C.Coy.) do. 19552 do. C. MILLS. (C.Coy.) do. 14330 do. A. ROSS. (C.Coy.) do. C. Coy. in Subsidiary trenches for the night.	

J. Fowler Capt.
10 Yorks. Regt.

21st Kurraun

10th Gyantshin
vols. 4

November 1915
121/7911

M Davis H.B.
11 sheets.

M.B.

Army Form C. 2118

WAR DIARY
or
INTELLIGENCE SUMMARY
(Erase heading not required.)

1o Yorkshire Regt.

Instructions regarding War Diaries and Intelligence Summaries are contained in F.S. Regs., Part II. and the Staff Manual respectively. Title Pages will be prepared in manuscript.

Sheet No. 1.

Place	Date	Hour	Summary of Events and Information	Remarks and references to Appendices
ARMENTIÈRES.	1915. Dec. 1.	—	In Billets at ARMENTIÈRES. Coy work and Route marches. D. Coy in Subsidiary trenches for the night.	
do.	2.	—	The Battn was inspected by Major General JACOB, Comdg. 2nd Division afternoon. Coy work etc. A. Coy in Subsidiary trenches for the night. 2nd Lieut. T.E.G. BAILEY reported for duty with the Battn.	
do.	3.	—	Provided working parties 200 strong for work in trenches. The Battn. paraded at 5.30 p.m. to relieve the 1st LINCOLN Regt. in trenches 74.75.76.77. The relief was completed at 6.40 p.m. The weather wet and windy. Nothing important to report.	
do.	4.	—	In trenches 74.75.76.77. A very wet night, not much work could be done. All communication trenches flooded. Nothing important reported, between 8.40 p.m. Dec 3 and 6 A.M. Dec 4. No. 19524 Pte. G. KERBY killed (A Coy). 20214 Pte. E. HEAWORTH wounded (A Coy). 13988 Pte. R.C. HUTCHINSON do. (A Coy).	
do.	5.	—	Clearing trenches, and pumping out communication trenches. There was a combined "Shoot" on the evening of the 4th: from trenches 76,77,78,79 & 80 with rifle and machine gun fire each 6th every 2 hrs & a feu de joie from 9 p.m. to 9.3 p.m. Nothing further important reported from 6 A.M. Dec 4 to 6 A.M. Dec 5. 2nd Lieut. W.H. HAYNES reported for duty with the Battn.	
do.	6.	—	Weather subsiding in PLANK Av. and JAPAN Rd. all very bad. Repairs being carried out in the firing trench. Nothing important reported from 6 A.M. Dec 5 to 6 A.M. Dec 6.	

WAR DIARY or INTELLIGENCE SUMMARY

Army Form C. 2118

10 Yorkshire Regt.   Sheet No 2

Place	Date	Hour	Summary of Events and Information	Remarks and references to Appendices
TRENCHES.	Dec 7.	—	In trenches 74, 75, 76, 77. water still going down but everything very sodden and repair work very bad. Got on with Battery impressions to + put from 6 am Dec 6. to 6 am Dec 7.	
do	8.	—	Wire retreating and repair work being carried on. There was an enormous Artillery strafe from 12 noon to 1 pm and very little reply from the Germans. 2nd Lieut H.V. DOVE (Acy) wounded 8614 Pte. T. BELL (SG) Killed 22789 R. FOXTON ,, wounded 19114 M. CLEVELAND ,, do. 18843 A.R. WARWICK ,, do. 19606 J. HAINES (AG) do. 15000 CAINE do.	
do	9	—	A very wet day. Not able to do much retaliating work about some level. A heavy bombardment on both sides during afternoon. The Battn. were relieved by the 1st Lincoln Regt. who took over the relief commenced at 4.45 pm and was completed at 7.25 pm. B.Coy took over a new Subsidiary Trench in the night. The Battn. went into billets at ARMENTIERES.	
ARMENTIERES	10.	—	In billets ARMENTIERES. Battn. cleaning up vicinity a working party of 100 men and 2 officers sent to work under R.E. at 1 pm. C Coyn Subsidiary Trenches for the night.	

10 Yorkshire Regt.   Army Form C. 2118

WAR DIARY
or
INTELLIGENCE SUMMARY
(Erase heading not required.)

Sheet No — 3.

Place	Date	Hour	Summary of Events and Information	Remarks and references to Appendices
ARMENTIERES	Dec 11	—	In Billets at ARMENTIERES. Inspection of Battn in marching order. Afternoon gum cleaned etc. Working parties as on the 10th.	
do.	12.	—	A. Coy in Subsidiary Trenches for the night. Working parties as on the 11th. Everything very quiet. D Coy in Subsidiary Trenches.	
do.	13.	—	C & L work and rout marches. Working parties as on the 12th. A. Shell burst in Batt. Billets. 18159 Pte. G.A. DAWSON. (A Coy) wounded 17475 Pte. D. KENNEDY. (D Coy) do. B. Coy in Subsidiary Trenches for the night. The Battn battery and Coy work.	
do.	14.	—	Lt. Col. ORAM 3rd Bn MANCHESTER Regt. and Lt Col WAYMAN. 3rd WEST RIDING Regt. attached for a tour of duty in the trenches. All quiet. C. Coy in Subsidiary trenches for the night. The Battn talking no parades.	
do.	15.	—	The Battn paraded at 4.30 pm in the Armentieres Sq: & 1st LINCOLN Regt in Rue Nationale 74.75.76.77. Relief commences 5 pm and was completed 8.15 pm. A bombardment by our Artillery took place during both morning & afternoon. 13459 Pte. C. SMITH (B Coy) wounded.	

Pl. C.SMITH

WAR DIARY
or
INTELLIGENCE SUMMARY

Army Form C. 2118

10 Yorkshire Regt.

Sheet No. —

Place	Date	Hour	Summary of Events and Information	Remarks and references to Appendices
Trenches	Dec 16.	—	In trenches 74, 75, 76, 77. The 63 Inf. Bgd. on our immediate right carried out a successful enterprise against the GERMAN trenches opposite to him at 3.00 A.M. The Bn. stood to be in case of Counter attack by none took place. We had some casualties from German bombardment during the night. 20286. Pte. R. BLENKINSOP (AG.) wounded 20312. „ H. HAW „ do 14242 „ T. ROBSON „ do 19614. „ J. H. NELSON „ do 14425. „ J. DICK (Dav.) do 19579. „ J. SMITH „ do 20312. „ F. SOLLITT „ do	
„	17.	—	a quiet day at night considerable bombing and some reinforcing 19195. Sgt. T. S. D. MADE (AG.) wounded 13100 Pte. J. ALLEN „ do 13582 „ N. REED „ do 20405 „ E. GREEN (SG) do 15521 „ J. H. FIRTH „ do	
„	18.	—	everything quiet. Work on Communication trenches and fire trenches going on satisfactorily, also were in front of parapet repairing entanglements. Capt. J. C. F. DOUGLAS. (AG.) wounded (since died of wounds) 11244 Pte. G. LIDDLE. (AG.) wounded	

WAR DIARY
or
INTELLIGENCE SUMMARY
(Erase heading not required.)

Army Form C. 2118

10. Yorkshire Regt.

Sheet No. 5.

Place	Date	Hour	Summary of Events and Information	Remarks and references to Appendices
Henches	Dec 19	—	In trenches 74. 75. 76. 77. a heavy bombardment by the GERMANS took place about 8. A.M. on all our trenches and supports and continued intermittently till about 11 A.M. our front line trench was damaged badly. Aerial Torpedoes were The retaliation from our artillery was very poor. There were five German airplanes up and not one of ours could be seen.	
			17461 Pte R. TORDISON (DoW) Killed	
			20324 a/L/Cpl F. BRYCE do	
			20358 Pte H.W. GRAY do	
			20262 a/L/Cpl T.H. PASHBY do	
			17798 Pte J. WILSON wounded	
			23189 " V.E. BARRY do	
			17543 " J. SMITH do	
			8849 Sgt A. TOSGOOD do	
			17492 a/Sgt H. McLELLAN do	
			8942 Sgt F. IGGO do	
			17564 Pte E. TREMBLE do	
			17567 " J. STOKER do	
			10516 " A. HUDSON (doy) do	
			13925 " J. RADFORD do	
			12070 " C.F. BARR (do) do	
			17649 Sgt A.F. GRIMBLE do	
			12469 Pte J. HARKER do	
			9046 " T. DOWSON (do) do	
			17538 " D. ROBERTSON do	
			13677 " A. FORD do In Hospital (suffering from Shock)	

Army Form C. 2118

1o Yorkshire Regt

WAR DIARY
or
INTELLIGENCE SUMMARY
(Erase heading not required.)

Sheet No. 6.

Instructions regarding War Diaries and Intelligence Summaries are contained in F.S. Regs., Part II. and the Staff Manual respectively. Title Pages will be prepared in manuscript.

Place	Date	Hour	Summary of Events and Information	Remarks and references to Appendices
Trenches	Dec 19	—	2nd Lieut D.M. EVANS and 2nd Lieut H. HUME reported for duty with the Batt.	
do.	20.	—	For trenches 74. 75. 76. 77. a very quiet day, very little shelling, able to get on with repair work to front line trenches.	
			12 NORTHUMBERLAND FUS. in trenches 78. 79. 80.	
			8. SOMERSET L.I. do. 71. 72. 73.	
do.	21.	—	A quiet day, repairs to front trenches continued. A bomb made by Arnest Johedsons on the 19th was about 6ft 8in by 2½ to 3½ft across the crater.	
			heavy Mr Hare arms who have been out for 3 mos. commenced to leave (?). This applies to the 2nd Division.	
			The Batt. were relieved by the 1st LINCOLN Regt. the relief began at 5pm. and was concluded at 9.30pm.	
			The Batt. went into Billets at ARMENTIERES.	
			A Coy in Subsidiary trenches for the night.	
ARMENTIERES.	22.	—	In Billets at ARMENTIERES. coming out of trenches the "Boch." machine guns were busy and called some casualties although very quiet.	
			The Batt. cleaning up and refitg.	
			15167 Cpl A. DUTCHMAN (C Coy) Hospital (Sick)	
			19520 Pte J. RUTTER (D Coy) Wounded	
			D Coy in Subsidiary trench for the night.	

WAR DIARY or **INTELLIGENCE SUMMARY**

Army Form C. 2118

1/0 Yorkshire Regt.   Sheet No. 1.

Place	Date	Hour	Summary of Events and Information	Remarks and references to Appendices
ARMENTIERES	Dec 23	—	In Billets at ARMENTIERES. inspection of billets at 10 A.M. and Baths in marching order afterward. Baths bathing and Coy work. B. Coy in Subsidiary trenches for the night. 4/4 trench and 1/5 trench run from I.5.C.1.1½ to I.5.C.9.9. 76 trench and 77 trench run from I.5.C.9.9 to I.5.A.5/4.7/4. (part of sheet 36) sheet 12. 1:10,000. 20423 Pte. W. NAYLOR (C Coy) wounded 21.12.15. 19520 Pte. T. RUTTER wounded on 12.12.15 died of wounds 23.12.15.	
do.	24.	—	Batt. bathing and Coy Drill &C. bombardment by English Lines did not hear much reply. 150 men sent on working parties to trenches. C Coy in Subsidiary trenches for the night.	
do.	25.	—	No parades, working party of 60 men sent to work in trenches. A Coy in Subsidiary trenches for the night, a bombardment going on during night and part of day. wounded from a battery direction.	
do.	26.	—	No parades working parties sent to trenches as usual, a quiet day D. Coy in Subsidiary trenches for the night	

WAR DIARY
INTELLIGENCE SUMMARY

10th York Regt Sheet No. 3

Army Form C. 2118

Place	Date	Hour	Summary of Events and Information	Remarks and references to Appendices
ARMENTIERES	27.12.15		Hostile Artillery in ARMENTIERES - Our Divisional and Heavy Artillery active in an arranged bombardment of enemy trenches at 12-45 pm. The Battalion relieved 14th Brigade in trenches 74 to 77 commencing at 4.30 pm. Relief completed at 7.15 pm. Casualties: 1st TABURIT "A" Coy wounded. Uneventful night.	
"	28.12.15		In trenches 74 to 77. Major Fowler proceeded on leave to England. Work repair & drainage work carried out, cleaning communication trenches etc. About 6 or 8 Whizzbangs put in our fire & support trenches 9.7 & 7.7. Also 9 or 10 shells into HOSPICE. Casualties 2290s Pte J. Scarfe 14330 Pte A Crouch "B"Coy Pte G Lawes W937 Pte H Bottes all wounded.	
"	29.12.15		In trenches 74 to 77. St Justin proceeded on leave. Trenches fine - water level dropped 2". Usual rifle fire cannot on - Trench sniper active on enemy's side fine & modern. Day quiet, unusual activity of enemy's rifle fire & machine guns at night.	
"	30.12.15		In trenches 74 to 77. Weather fine. Enemy quiet but between 1 & 2 enemy "crumped" Peril & Pd Wd. trench with his heavy crumps out. Between 3 & 4 pm he put 6 or 8 Whizbangs into fire and support trenches and about 4.30 snarked front in front of A Coy H.Q with shrapnel. Casualties 19636 Pte Armstrong A W "A" Coy wounded 14131 " Swift W. H " " 13322 4/04 Storry J B " B " 12305 Marsh L A " 19209 Pte Joyce A " 8546 Sgt Chapman S "	

Army Form C. 2118

WAR DIARY
or
INTELLIGENCE SUMMARY
(Erase heading not required.)

10th York Regt.   Sheet No. 8

Place	Date	Hour	Summary of Events and Information	Remarks and references to Appendices
Armentieres	31st		At 2.15 am an enemy patrol of 3 men penetrated our wires in front of listening post at House 6, and, undemand by our 9th post fired on and wounded the 2 sentries. They escaped in the darkness. Weather fine but blustering. Wounded: No. 17508 Pte Wood's S.W. "D" Coy. Wounded. " 20343 " Watson J At 11 pm enemy opened heavy rifle & machine gun fire on our parapet to which we replied — casualties nil.	
	31/12/15			E.B. Fadwicks Lt Colonel Cmdg 10th York Regt.

10th Yorks Reg
Vol 6

21st Div

62 Bde

10# books.
vol. 5
Ten

Army Form C. 2118

WAR DIARY
or
INTELLIGENCE SUMMARY
(Erase heading not required.)

10th YORK Regt.   Sheet I

Place	Date	Hour	Summary of Events and Information	Remarks and references to Appendices
ARMENTIERS	1915 Jan 1st		In Trenches 74 to 77. A quiet day. Weather blustering. A few enemy shells but no mean Quality Row. Enemy machine guns opened fire at 8-45 earlier than usual. Usual repairs and drainage work carried out in fire, support and communication trenches.	
	Jan 2nd		Enemy shelled fire and support trenches with whizz bangs between 10 & 11 - also House 6. Desultory m.g. shelled with 15 cm - 8 shells. At junction of 77 & 78 in German parapet opposite enemy erected a file with iron later on top; placing on his parapet on each side of pile two oblong black wooden boxes of about 4'x 2½' and the other 2'x 2'. Casualty No 20242 Pte J. Brown "D" Coy - wounded. Relieved by 1st Lincoln Regt - Relief complete at 11.20 pm. Casualties 20337 Pte G. Horsman "D" Coy wounded - No 12937 Pte E. Atkinson "B" wounded	
	Jan 3rd		In huts in Armentiers - day spent in cleaning up - enemy quiet. Usual working parties at night. "C" Coy Subaltern's line - to ELM Avenue - "A" working parties.	
	Jan 4th		In huts in Armentiers - CO's inspection of huts & Coys out on duty - Usual working parties. B Coy D. 6pm. Inspection of packs of A Coy 2-30 pm. "D" Coy weakly. Casualties Pte S. Charlton "B" Killed. " L McKinney " wounded " A Pallin " " A Coy Subaltern's line - B Coy Elm Avenue	

Army Form C. 2118

WAR DIARY or INTELLIGENCE SUMMARY

(Erase heading not required.)

10th York R[egiment]. Sheet II

Place	Date	Hour	Summary of Events and Information	Remarks and references to Appendices
Armentieres	Jany 5th		In billets — Usual fatigues & working parties C Coy 6 am B. Coy 6 pm. "B" Coy Subsiding line. A. Coy Coln Reserve. Lieut MILNE proceeded on leave.	
"	Jany 6th		In billets — Usual working parties A Coy 6 am. C Coy 6 pm. Washing & bathing remainder. "B" Coy Subsiding line — "D" Coln Reserve. Capt FOWLER returned from leave.	
"	7th		In billets. Usual working parties. a very quiet day. C. Coy in Subsidiary trenches.	
"	8th		In billets — a quiet day. no parades. working parties as usual. The Battn. relieved the 1 LINCOLNS. in trenches 74-77 relief completed at 8.00 pm. Lieut. GOATER. returned from leave. 19639 Pte. R. SCOTT. (D Coy.) Killed	
"	9th		In trenches 74-77. nothing important reported from 8.00 pm on 8th to 6 am on 9th. about 12.30 PM. the enemy (Batteries) trench 77 which about 20 shells did a little damage. 11303 Pte. T. FREEMAN. (C Coy.) Killed. 20403 Pte. H. JOHNSON. (C) wounded. Lieut HOLLINGSWORTH. went on leave	
"	10.		do fine weather. & water getting away. work in progress on entrances heavy artillery (we hear) to our N. presumably, near YPRES.	

WAR DIARY or **INTELLIGENCE SUMMARY**

Army Form C. 2118

Yorkshire Regt. Sheet 3

Place	Date	Hour	Summary of Events and Information	Remarks and references to Appendices
ARMENTIERES	Jan 11	-	In trenches 34-44 nothing important reported between 6AM on 10th and 11th. Usual work in trenches carried out. At 11AM on artillery carried out a bombardment on enemy trenches 20. Having special attention to the enemy's wire in preparation for cutting out scheme to take place at 11-15pm on Jan 11. The enemy replied on our front line doing slight damage. At 10.15pm the Batn. was to arms whilst the R.W.F. carried out their appreciation. Lieut. & 2/Lt. CUMMINGS } went on leave. Capt. & Chapln. PARSONS }	
"	12.	do	Our artillery opened at 11-15pm on the 11th. and continued till 11-40pm whilst our infantry were firing. On the enemy replied causing us several casualties. It is reported that 3 German prisoners went to join us as a spy went to kill the night of the 11th was perfectly quiet after the outbreak. Capt. ELKINGTON (R.A.M.C.) went on leave.	

9248 Pte. C. KEATING (D) wounded
17126 " J.W. ELTRINGHAM (B) killed
12612 " W. APPLETON B do
20335 " W. ELIOTT C wounded
12671 " C. MILLET C do
16709 " J. LAWS A do
12876 " W. BRUCE A do
13436 " J. HETHERINGTON A do
17342 " G. WILSON C sick

Army Form C. 2118

WAR DIARY
or
INTELLIGENCE SUMMARY
(Erase heading not required.)

10 Yorkshire Regt. Sheet 4

Place	Date	Hour	Summary of Events and Information	Remarks and references to Appendices
ARMENTIERES	Jan/13	—	In trenches 74-77 a very quiet day, very little shellfire, work on trenches as usual, endeavour to get our wire well strengthened, weather .... 15026 Pte H.B. Fox wounded.	
"	14	—	2 Lieut. GARDINER returned from leave. 2 do PRATT do do. Do. artillery quiet, little shellfire. Plank Av. Rd. being completed, wire and other communication trenches cleaned. The Batt. was relieved by 1 LINCOLNS relief completed about 9.30 pm do to went into billets at ARMENTIERES.	
"	15	—	In billets at ARMENTIERES. Lieut MILNE returned from leave as paradis Batts cleaning usual working parties on to trenches. D Coy in Subsidiary trenches.	
"	16	—	do. 20280 Pte T. WOOD (am) killed 19514 J. BARNBROOK B. wounded 14762 L/Cpl. T. HIGGINS B. do 12989 Pte J.W. LACKENBY C. do During the night 15/16 the enemy bombarded the Town intermittently returned about 12.45 am afterwards all very quiet. B Coy in Subsidiary trenches.	
"	17	—	do. do. Col work and Batt.n bakery on Key pontoon as usual sent up to trenches. C Coy in Subsidiary trenches.	

WAR DIARY or INTELLIGENCE SUMMARY

Army Form C. 2118

Sheet 5.

10 1/0 Rohan Regt

Place	Date	Hour	Summary of Events and Information	Remarks and references to Appendices
ARMENTIERES	Jan 18.	—	In Billets at ARMENTIERES. Batt. bathing & harassaday after windies, also Stratting Colony coops, about 7-10 p.m. an heavy fire in the over but over a short 12 s.h.m. in cops preceding indictions of some PROFESSIONAL.	
"	19	—	do. A few shots during marches. Coy broke and bathing as arrived, quiet day or being reported.	
"	20	—	do. D Coy in Subsidiary trenches A/Lieut. HOLLINGSWORTH returned from leave. 2/Lt CRADDOCK wounded on parade during the early part of the day, a little shelling by enemy Recd Capt PARSONS returned from leave.	
"	21	—	In trenches 74-77 trenches much drier, and work going on satisfactorily. 7B and A/188 relief 9.10pm. The Batt. relieved 1 LINCOLN Regt. in trenches 74-77 relief complete 2.10am nothing important reported between 9.10pm and 2am. 2am no 2101.	
"	22	—	do. Still fine weather. Very warm. Work as usual, enemy's artillery more active, and caused some casualties.	

Capt. ELKINGTON. (R.A.M.C) returned from leave   2nd Lt W.H. LLEWELLYN
reported for duty with Batt. and was posted to D.G.   2nd Lieut C.A.M. BUTCHER
reported for duty with Batt. and was posted to A.Coy.

18747 Pte J.W. ROXBY.   (D) wounded
12702   "   T. ROBINSON.   D   do.
19660   "   T. BEACON.   A.   do.
16590   "   T. RIDLEY   A.   do.
17385   "   W. CORRUTHERS   A.   killed
13774 C/Sgt T. CROGGINS   D.   wounded
14578 Pte A.M. WATSON.   D.   shock

WAR DIARY or INTELLIGENCE SUMMARY

Army Form C. 2118

10 Yorkshire Regt.   Sheet 6.

Place	Date	Hour	Summary of Events and Information	Remarks and references to Appendices
ARMENTIERES	Jan 23	—	In trenches 74-77 a very quiet day, very little shelling, and a good deal of air work [observation being done]. Repairs to trenches being further proceeded with.	
"	24	—	do. a heavy bombardment of enemy's wire trenches opposite, commenced at 11.30 a.m. About 1 hour clearing work proceeded with. Pt. J.T. OLIVER A Coy wounded.	
"	25	—	do. Lieut. BARRACLOUGH returned from leave. Artillery on both sides active all day. Train work being carried out. The following promotions were Gazetted on Jan 15.	
			Capt V. FOWLER to be ? Major.	
			Lieut. R.M. MILNE " Capt.	
			2.Lieut W.R. KNOTT " Lieut.	
			do T.SYLVESTER " do	
"	26.	—	Subsidiary were carried out to the N. of the Railway and at the MUSHROOM (Inf 63 Bde) at about 9.55 p.m. Artillery active on both sides, but able to carry on with work. The Battn. were relieved by 1st LINCOLNS and returned to Billets in ARMENTIERES. B. Coy in Subsidiary trenches.	
			19407 Pte. J. CHAMBERS (C Coy) killed.	
			20415 " R.P. DIMMON A do	
			12201 " E. NEWTON. C wounded	
			14459 " R. WALTON. C do	
			15534 " W.L. JOHNSON. A do	

Army Form C. 2118

WAR DIARY or INTELLIGENCE SUMMARY

(Erase heading not required.)

10 Yorkshire Regt   Sheet 4.

Place	Date	Hour	Summary of Events and Information	Remarks and references to Appendices
ARMENTIERES	Jan 27	—	In billets at ARMENTIERES. No parades. Wet & very showery. A quiet day in the Town. Batt. bathing on Hd. cleaning. C. Coy in subsidiary trenches. B. " " " " 15510 Pte W. ARCHIBALD 18286 " J. WARDLE (K) Killed 7365 " F. BRADLEY (W) wounded Lieut CRADDOCK returned from leave.	
"	28	—	do. during the night of 27/28 the enemy heavily shelled the front line trenches which was replied to by our guns. In the evening were relieved. The Battn. standing to arms. D Coy in the Subsidiary trenches. 2nd Lieut PARKER went on leave	
"	29	—	do. a very quiet day in the Town Coy work and working parties. A Coy in subsidiary trenches.	
"	30	—	do. no parades except church D. Coy in subsidiary trenches	
"	31	—	do. Coy work &c. usual working parties sent to trenches. a quiet day. C Coy in Subsidiary trenches.	

W. B. Edwards Lt Col
Comdg 10th York Regt

Army Form C. 2118

WAR DIARY
or
INTELLIGENCE SUMMARY
(Erase heading not required.)

10 Yorkshire Regt.   Sheet No. 1.

Place	Date 1916	Hour	Summary of Events and Information	Remarks and references to Appendices
ARMENTIERES.	Feb. 1	—	In Billets at ARMENTIERES. Coy work and working parties as usual. a very quiet day.	
			D. Coy in Subsidiary Trenches.	
			20425 Pte. F. HANSON (C.G.) wounded.	
			2062? " P. SMITH. do.	
do.	2	—	do. Coy work, working parties as usual. a quiet day.	
			A. Coy in Subsidiary trenches.	
do.	3	—	do. do.	
do.	4	—	do. B. Coy in Subsidiary trench.	
			working parties provided.	
			C. Coy in Subsidiary Trenches.	
			2nd Lieut. HAIGH returns from leave.	
do.	5	—	do. working parties as usual.	
			D. Coy in Subsidiary Trenches.	
			Lieut. SYLVESTER returns from leave.	
do.	6	—	do. working parties as usual. a quiet day.	
			A. Coy in Subsidiary Trenches.	
			Lieut. SUCH goes on leave	
			2nd Lieut. BALL do.	
			Lieut. GOATER promoted to Captain.	
			2nd " SUCH " " Lieut.	

Army Form C. 2118

WAR DIARY
or
INTELLIGENCE SUMMARY
(Erase heading not required.)

10 Yorkshire Regt. Sheet No 2.

Instructions regarding War Diaries and Intelligence Summaries are contained in F. S. Regs., Part II. and the Staff Manual respectively. Title Pages will be prepared in manuscript.

Place	Date	Hour	Summary of Events and Information	Remarks and references to Appendices
ARMENTIERES	Feb. 7	—	In billets at ARMENTIERES. no parade. The Battn relieves the 4th MIDDLESEX Regt in trenches, 72, 73, 74, 75, 76, 77. The relief commenced at 6.45 pm and was completed at 8.20 pm. 2nd Lieut PARKER returned from leave	
do.	8	—	In trenches, 72 - 77. a very quiet day, men preparing & altering trenches in accordance with new scheme of defence. 20040 L/Cpl H. SIMPSON. (DCo.) wounded. 8864 Pte T. BENBOW. C. Killed. 18940 " E.S. GLASPER. D. wounded. 2nd Lieut. LLEWELLYN went on leave.	
do.	9	—	do. continuation of work making new strong points, a quiet day.	
do.	10	—	do. work on strong points continued, and on clearing Communication trenches. The enemy's Artillery was active all day RANK AV QUALITY ROW, and DISTILLERY shelled. 2nd Lieut HUME returned from leave	
do.	11	—	do. a very wet day, and water rising, work on strong points, carried on. Enemy's Artillery still active. 2nd Lieut A. DICKENSON reported for duty with the Battn, and was posted to D Coy. 2nd Lieut COLLIER returned from leave.	

1875 Wt. W593/826 1,000,000 4/15 J.B.C. & A. A.D.S.S./Forms/C. 2118.

WAR DIARY or **INTELLIGENCE SUMMARY**

Army Form C. 2118

10 Yorkshire Regt. Sheet No 3.

Place	Date	Hour	Summary of Events and Information	Remarks and references to Appendices
ARMENTIÈRES	Feb/12.	—	In trenches 1/2-4/1 The enemy shelled S.P.X. and PLANK Av. near old Battn. H.Q. with H.E. from big calibre Howitzers, and made good shooting, about 50 shells were fired. Considerable damage done to S.P.X. 14293 Pte. G. WILSON. (AG) wounded. 20338 " W. HOPE. (B) Killed. 2nd Lieut. SLATER. went on leave. At 5.15 p.m. there was a M.M.G and smoke bomb demonstration against the trenches opposite trenches 78-80. The enemy retaliated with T.M. and 4.5" H.R. and caused no some casualties, afterwards the night was quiet. 2nd Lieut. PARKER. (D6.) wounded 14538. Pte. A. BLACK. D. do 14392. " J. DOCKERTY. D. do 22944 " S. PEARSON D. do 20491 " J.E. CLAYTOR D. do 14073 L/Cpl. G. PAXTON. D. do 13724 Pte. J. THIRWELL B. do 14316 " B. MARSTERMAN C. do 20341 " J. COLEMAN C. shock.	

WAR DIARY or INTELLIGENCE SUMMARY

(Erase heading not required.)

Army Form C. 2118

1o Yorkshire Regt.   Sheet No 4.

Place	Date	Hour	Summary of Events and Information	Remarks and references to Appendices
ARMENTIERES.	3/4/13	—	Our trenches 42-44 artillery on both sides not so active, everything else as usual. The Battn was relieved by 1st LINCOLN Regt (relief was completed at 9.0 pm) and went into the Subsidiary trenches to relieve the 13th NORTHUMBLD. FUSLRS. The relief of Subsidiary trenches was completed at 10.45 pm. 19534. Pte. J.T. WRIGHT. (D.G.) wounded. 20319. " A. McBEAN D. " died of wounds. 2nd Lieut BASS went on leave.	
do.	14.	—	In Subsidiary trenches from LILLE Rd. to FME. de LA BUTERNE. a quiet night, the enemy commenced shelling some old Gun positions about 10 A.M. and then lifted and shelled the ground between CHAPELLE. ARMENTIERES, and RUE. MARLE and did some damage to Communication trench leading from Subsidiary trenches back to ARMENTIERES. the shelling was continued in the afternoon. Lieut. G.C.R. RANSOME reported for duty with the Battn and was posted to D. Coy. 2nd Lieut. W.E. MATTHEWS. reported for duty with the Battn and was posted to C. Coy. Lieut. SUCH. returned from leave.	

WAR DIARY or INTELLIGENCE SUMMARY

Army Form C. 2118

10 Yorkshire Regt.   Sheet No 5.

Place	Date	Hour	Summary of Events and Information	Remarks and references to Appendices
ARMENTIERES.	Feb 15	—	In Subsidiary trenches (as before) slight Artillery activity over our sector, more to the north. Working parties supplied to trenches. 2nd Lieut. BALL returned from leave.	
do.	16.	—	do. a very quiet day. The Batt. were relieved by the 12th NORTHUMBLD. FUSRS. The relief was completed at 4.20 p.m. The Batt. went into Billets at ARMENTIERES.	
do.	17.	—	In billets at ARMENTIERES. a quiet day, the Batt. cleaning and bathing. 2nd Lieut. JARDINE went on leave.	
do.	18.	—	do. a quiet day working parties sent to trenches.	
do.	19.	—	do. 2nd Lieut CHAMBERLAIN went on leave.	
do.	20.	—	do. a quiet day, no parades, provided a working party of 500 men for day & night work.	
do.	21.	—	do. a quiet day working parties as before. 2nd Lieut SLATER returned from leave.	
do.	22.	—	do. a quiet day, with a snow storm in morning, working parties sent to trenches as usual.	
do.	23.	—	do. Same as on 22nd. 2nd Lieut BUTCHER went on leave.	

Army Form C. 2118

WAR DIARY
or
INTELLIGENCE SUMMARY

(Erase heading not required.)

10 Yorkshire Regt.   Vol. 1 to 6.

Place	Date	Hour	Summary of Events and Information	Remarks and references to Appendices
ARMENTIÈRES	Feb 24	—	On 11th at ARMENTIÈRES a quiet day. At 11pm D Coy of the Battn undertook an enterprise against BLACK R. REDOUBT, a portion of the enemy's trench opposite 70.14 trench. The party (who had been training for the enterprise) consisted of 5 officers and 45 men. The officers were Capt MILNE, Lieut RANSOME, Lieut COLLIER, 2nd Lieut CRADDOCK and Lieut DICKINSON. The object of the enterprise was to obtain prisoners, kill Germans, ascertain if any gas apparatus had been installed in this sector, and do general damage. The attack was unfortunately detected, and our men were bombed by the enemy as they were getting over the enemy's wire, causing a number of casualties and forcing our party to retire without having carried out their object.	
			Lieut G.C. RANSOME (DG) wounded. 2nd Lieut V.D. CRADDOCK (CG) serious wound.	
			M513 Sgt. COLLIER do. 14377 Pte. W. CLARKE (DG) wounded.	
			18638 L/Cpl. J. HALL do. d. 22969 " J.G. LUNN do do	
			17344 Pte. J. STEPHENSON do. do. 20562 " A. ANDERSON do do	
			17553 " C. SIMPSON do. do. 20391 " S. GLOVER do do	
			17594 " A. WEBSELL do.	
			9429 Cpl. H. COLLIER do. missing	
			19544 Pte M.H. LIDDLE do do	
			19942 " J.W. BARKER do do	

WAR DIARY
or
INTELLIGENCE SUMMARY

Army Form C. 2118

Title Pages 10 Yorkshire Regt. Sheet No. 4.

Place	Date	Hour	Summary of Events and Information	Remarks and references to Appendices
ARMENTIÈRES	3/25	—	In Billets at ARMENTIERES. a quiet day, cold & freezing. The Batt relieved the 4th MIDDLESEX. Regt. in trenches 83 to 89. The relief commenced at 4 p.m. and was completed at 9.25 p.m.	
do.	26	—	In trenches 83 to 89. a quiet day, very cold, and more snow fell during the night. The work of repair being carried on in accordance with scheme. 20323 Pte. P. RYAN (A Coy) Killed. 14602 " M. LAHENEN (C) wounded seriously. Trenches 83 to 89 run from C. 23. c. 2.9. to C. 16. d. e. 9.	
do.	27	—	do 2nd Lieut JARDINE returned from leave.	
do	28	—	do a quiet day except for a few shells in HOUPLINES. The trenches are rather wet, during to the frost breaking, work being carried on, repairing the parapet in rear of march and abating communication trenches, some artillery activity on both sides, not much damage. 2nd Lieut CHAMBERLAIN returned from leave.	
do	29	—	do artillery active and had about 12 shells near Batty H.Q. but no damage, wind on N side of IRISH AV. going on well. 12201 Pte. E. NEWTON. (C Coy) wounded 19042 " A.H. ROBINSON (B) do.	

March 1st 1916.   W.R. Wilson Lt Col.
Comdg 10th Yorks Regt

62

10 York Reg
Vol 7

T.B.

Army Form C. 2118

WAR DIARY
or
INTELLIGENCE SUMMARY
(Erase heading not required.)

1/6 Yorkshire Regt.   Sheet No. 1.

Instructions regarding War Diaries and Intelligence Summaries are contained in F.S. Regs., Part II. and the Staff Manual respectively. Title Pages will be prepared in manuscript.

Place	Date	Hour	Summary of Events and Information	Remarks and references to Appendices
ARMENTIÈRES.	1915 Jan. 1.	—	In trenches 83-89 trenches rather wet and river still rising. a quiet night. during night a patrol went out in front of trench 84. to try and obtain information about new work that appeared to be going on in front of German lines. The patrol got close to the German trenches, and found a good deal of work going on in front of their parapet. the working parties being protected by men in rifle pits. one of have rifleman retired on approach of our patrol. and a pair of German gloves were found in the pit.	
do.	2.	—	at about 4.30 a.m. a heavy fire was noticed to the N. shells could be seen bursting, and during the morning news came that the British to the N. had had a success. our trenches very wet, and some of the communication trenches flooded. The Battn. was relieved by the 1st LINCOLN Regt the relief commenced at 6.30 p.m. and was completed at 9.5 p.m. The Battn went into Brigade reserve in the village of HOUPLINES.	Major SHAND. B Co. wounded.
HOUPLINES	3	—	In billets in HOUPLINES a very quiet day working parties supplied.	
do	4.	—	a very quiet day round the billets with the exception of some shelling at HOUPLINES CHURCH. also heavy shells were heard going towards ARMENTIÈRES more inland.	
do	5.	—	no parade. working parties sent up to trenches. a quiet day	
do	6.	—	working parties as usual. a very quiet day some or our	

Army Form C. 2118

WAR DIARY
or
INTELLIGENCE SUMMARY
(Erase heading not required.)

10 Yorkshire Regt.   Sheet No 2.

Place	Date	Hour	Summary of Events and Information	Remarks and references to Appendices
HOUPLINES	May 7	—	In billets in HOUPLINES. Working parties as usual, a very quiet day, more snow, the remainder of Battn. sandbagging billets and strutting cellars in case of bombardment.	
			Lieut J.N. BARRACLOUGH promoted Captn.	
			2nd Lieut N.E.S. GARDINER " Lieut.	
do.	8.	—	do. V.D.K. CRADDOCK " "	
			About 3" of rain fell during the night, a very quiet day, and river badly in flood. The Battn was relieved at 9.30 pm by the 10. K.O.Y.L.I. Regt. and went into billets in ARMENTIERES.	
ARMENTIERES	9.	—	ARMENTIERES Battn cleaning and bathing, working parties supplies for trenches	
do.	10.	—	do Battn. in close reserve, a quiet day	
do.	11.	—	do working parties sent same strength (300) as usual, a quiet day	
do.	12.	—	do working parties no usual, no other parades.	
			Capt. J.S. CRONE reported for duty with the Battn from photos to B.Q.	
			2nd Lieut S.J. KINNACH do D. "	
			do S. LOVEL — do D. "	
do.	13.	—	do fine weather again and river falling, a very quiet day, hardly any shelling at all	

Army Form C. 2118

WAR DIARY
or
INTELLIGENCE SUMMARY
(Erase heading not required.)

10 Yorkshire Regt. Sheet No 3.

Place	Date	Hour	Summary of Events and Information	Remarks and references to Appendices
ARMENTIERES	Mar 14.	—	On billets in ARMENTIERES. A very quiet day, very hot. The Battn. relieved the 8th SOMERSET Regt. and 4th MIDDLESEX Regt. in trenches 73 – 77. The relief was completed at 8.50.p.m.	
"	15.	—	In trenches 73 – 77 a quiet day. There appeared to have been considerable enemy shelling in the Communication trenches since we last occupied the trenches.	
"	16.	do.	Machine guns active during night. During the afternoon several 7.7 shells were sent over trenches 76, 77, and caused up some causalities, otherwise all quiet. Weather all the fine, and wiring, revetting, allowing work to be carried on in all trenches and communication trenches.	
			7369. Pte. C. SIMPSON. (3.G.) wounded. 13.3.16.
			17529. A/Cpl H. BEAY. D. do. 15.3.16
			22873. L/Cpl. C. LONG. B. Killed. 16.3.16
			8921. Cpl. S.M. J. HIGGINS. B. wounded.
			19196. L/Cpl. J.H. CORRIE. B. do.
			17955. Pte. T. WELSH. B. do.
"	17.	do.	Some shell fire, but on the whole quiet.
			14346. Pte. S. ARMSTRONG. D. Killed.
			9329. Sgt. J.T. CRUDDACE. D. wounded.
			23799. Pte. H. SAWYER. D. do.
			15542. " H. COOPER. A. do.

Army Form C. 2118

WAR DIARY
or
INTELLIGENCE SUMMARY
(Erase heading not required.)

Sheet No. 4

10 Yorkshire Regt.

Place	Date	Hour	Summary of Events and Information	Remarks and references to Appendices
ARMENTIÈRES	May 18.	—	In trenches 73-77. Our artillery active in morning, trenches trying to shell and work going on as usual. Retrenchment and 73 S. going on well. At 6.30 pm our trench mortars bombarded the enemy lines opposite trench 80, with good result. 20605 Pte. P. PRYKE (B. wounded).	
"	19.	—	do. At 6.30 a.m. the enemy opened a heavy bombardment of trenches 79, 80, 77½, (or for as could be seen) and their supports probably in retaliation for the damage done on the evening the 18th. The bombardment continued till about 4-15 A.M., and with only very slight casualties. The remainder of the day was quiet except for the usual artillery and a few of grenades. 13640. Pte. J. W. STUBBS. (A) wounded. 20230. " B. KEMP. (A) do. 23469. " J. RICE. (B) do. 17401. " A. P. DUNCAN. (D) do. 17524. " T. PARK. (D) do. 79.11. " J. WIDDERFIELD. (A) do. 10431. " S. ROSS. (B) do. 13375. " J. CUTHBERTSON. (D) killed.	
	20.	—	do. Work going on as usual, a quiet day, except for slight artillery activity chiefly on own side.	

Army Form C. 2118

WAR DIARY or INTELLIGENCE SUMMARY

(Erase heading not required.)

10 Yorkshire Regt   Sheet No 5

Place	Date	Hour	Summary of Events and Information	Remarks and references to Appendices
ARMENTIERES	21	—	In trenches 73-77 about 8 A.M. the enemy opposite trenches 79 & 80 sent over a number of Shrapnel. Our guns 4 hours replied suitably, otherwise a very quiet day. The Battn were relieved in trenches by the 10th LANCASHIRE FUSILIERS of the 51st Brigade, and 17th Division, the relief being completed at 10 p.m. The Battn went into billets for the night in ARMENTIERES.	
"	22	—	The Battn formed up in ARMENTIERES at 7.45 A.M. (ready to move off) and marched to STEENWERCKE into new billets arriving there at 10 A.M. The billets were in barns etc. and 1½ Coys in canvas huts. Platoon Offrs. and Battn training to commence at once.	
STEENWERCKE	23	—	In billets. Battn cleaning and drilling. Platoon drill etc.	
do.	24	—	do. Bathing & Coy work during the night about 2 in of snow fell.	
do.	25	—	do. in morning Coy training. The Battn was inspected by the Commander in Chief at 2.40 p.m. after inspection Battn marched back to billets.	
do.	26	—	In billets. Church parade no other work. Lt. Col. EDDOWES went on leave and Major FOWLER took over command during his absence	
do.	27	—	do. Company training. B. Coy training at Brigade bombing school. A. Coy inoculated against PARA. TYPHOID. 2nd Lieut. V. B. ELLIOTT absent from duty, has been posted to A. Coy.	

WAR DIARY
or
INTELLIGENCE SUMMARY

(Erase heading not required.)

10 Yorkshire Regt.

Army Form C. 2118

Sheet No. 6.

Place	Date	Hour	Summary of Events and Information	Remarks and references to Appendices
STERNWERCKE	Mar 28.	—	On billets. Company training. B. Coy Inoculated. Inspection at 11.40 A.M. by Gen. PLUMMER commanding 2nd ARMY, one by how each Battn in the Brigade. The General wishes the men all good wishes on their going to a new Area and Army.	
do.	29.	—	Company training. C. Coy M.G. Inoculated. Major S.W.E. SHAND went on leave. Capt. McLELLAN re-joined the Battn for duty and took over command of C. Coy from Capt GOATER.	
do.	30.	—	Company training and bathing. Orders arrived for us to move on April 1st. Inoculation suspended until arrival in new area.	
do.	31.	—	Company training, also packing up for move. The Battn moved away from the General billeting area to entrain at BAILLEUL. Moving off at 10 p.m. The Transport and one Coy (A) having moved off at 6 p.m. The entraining was completed at 12.8 A.M. Apr 1.16. Train left BAILLEUL station at 12.8 A.M. Apr 1.16.	

W. Morley Major. A.C.
O.C. 10 Yorkshire Regt.

WAR DIARY or INTELLIGENCE SUMMARY

Army Form C. 2118

10th York Regt. Vol 8

J.B.

Place	Date	Hour	Summary of Events and Information	Remarks and references to Appendices
Field	April			
	2nd-6th		Bn arrived at LONGEAU (AMIENS) 11 am & marched to CARDONETTE went into billets about 3 pm. Reported quiet weather fine	
	7th-8th		In billets at CARDONETTE. Route marching, instruction in bombing etc. "C" Coy a HEILLY for work on Railway siding. Battalion inoculated against para Typhoid	
	8th		2/Lt BROWN reported for duty – posted to B Coy – Regt Sports at 3 pm.	
	15th		10.30 am Battalion marched to LA NEUVILLE arriving 1–15 pm. Remaining till 15th	
			11 am Battalion marched to Ville sous Corbie arriving 2–30 pm. Between 6 & 7 pm village shelled with 14 5.9" shells from FRICOURT. Bn went into billets	
	11th to 20th		In billets at Ville – Working parties daily 600–800 men on preparatory work. Wiring night & day	
	20th		Battalion relieved 8th Somerset L.I. in left sect of Dorset front from 7.2.6 10.6½ to 27.2.20. marching through MEAULTE. 200 yds between platoons en route. Reached 17 from Ville 2 pm. Relief complete 7.15 pm. Ruined steadily from 3–30 to 9 pm. Capt. Jellcorn appointed Town Major LA NEUVILLE	

WAR DIARY 10th YORK Rgt.
INTELLIGENCE SUMMARY

Army Form C. 2118

Place	Date	Hour	Summary of Events and Information	Remarks and references to Appendices
Field	April 22nd contd.	9-15 pm	Stokesmortar carried out by R.I. Rifles on our left covered by heavy bombardment of enemy trenches. Enemy retaliated with bombardment of our trenches particularly on "C" Coy front, causing casualties 1 killed, 3 wounded. A bomb exploded on its way to trenches causing following casualties 5 wounded.	
	23rd		Sgt Trimble - Enemy shell about 4-30 pm caused following casualties 2Lt Hague C.S.M. Howarth, 2 Pte Hunter "C" Coy wounded - first two severely	
	24th	11 pm	Sgt Trimble - At 11 pm enemy heavily bombarded "A" Coy trenches at PURFLEET with Sausages (Minenwerfer) Canisters (Trench Mortars) and Shells of various calibres causing 5 casualties. 2Lt Alexandre & Lt Cornaby joined battalion. James posted to B. Eaton to C.	
	25th		Artillery on both sides active - about 8 pm enemy activity increased - Combardant of A Coy trenches with rifle grenades. Casualties Sgt Lockham & 2 men wounded.	
	26th		Enemy artillery very active all day with 10 & 15 cm shells into Kings Coys Reconaissances 4 men wounded.	

WAR DIARY of 10th YORK R/f.
INTELLIGENCE SUMMARY

Army Form C. 2118

(Erase heading not required.)

Place	Date	Hour	Summary of Events and Information	Remarks and references to Appendices
Field	Ap 27		In trenches. Enemy artillery and trench mortars very active on front line and supports. Our artillery carried out heavy bombardment of enemy trenches in front of TAMBOUR. At 9-50 pm Cpl Toes & 6 men endeavoured to enter enemy trench opposite "C" Coys salient – enemy too much alert – our casualties one fatal	
	28th		In trenches – unintermittent bombardment by enemy of our trenches with trench mortars, canister, & rifle grenades.	
	29th		In trenches – At 4 pm a trench mortar appeared in "C" Coys front & fired 4 rounds into supports. Our 18 pr fired 6 rounds HE into position direct by Lt Bailey & trench mortar did not fire again.	
	30th		At 2-15 am Enemy began very heavy bombardment of our trenches & support and communication trenches which lasted till 3-15 am – "Bulletin" stated 5" Trenches badly damaged in places – especially PURFLEET. During dark enemy attempted raid on trenches on our right (12th N.F.)	

Army Form C. 2118

WAR DIARY of 10th York Regt
or
INTELLIGENCE SUMMARY

(Erase heading not required.)

Place	Date	Hour	Summary of Events and Information	Remarks and references to Appendices
Field	April 30th		Attack repulsed, & two enemy prisoners taken. A Coy of ???? men badly damaged. Lt Jardine severely wounded. At 7-30 pm a 5am enemy carried out very heavy bombardment of our trenches lasting till 9 pm, principally in "A" Coy in PURFLEET. Our artillery replied with barrage on enemy front line which effectually prevented any contemplated raid. Casualties 1 man killed 1 Officer 2 N.C.O.s & 11 men wounded. Men behaved wonderfully well throughout —	

Co P Osborne Lt Col
Comdg 10th York R

Army Form C. 2118

WAR DIARY
or
INTELLIGENCE SUMMARY
(Erase heading not required.)

10 Yorkshire Regt.   63/31   Sheet No. 1. Vol 4

Place	Date	Hour	Summary of Events and Information	Remarks and references to Appendices
MEAULTE.	May 1.	—	In trenches, a quiet morning. Throughout the night there were occasional bursts of shrapnel from the enemy on our front line & Sap heads. 7.0.2/1.2c at X.26.d.0.5. These bursts were replied to by our guns. 13824 Pte. W. SIMPSON (A) wounded. 18174 " E. PRYCE (A) do. Capt. PARSONS proceeded on leave. Lieut W.E. MATTHEWS proceeded on a M.G. course to CAMIERS.	
do.	2.	—	A quiet morning. The Battn was relieved by the 10th K.O.Y.L.I. The relief commenced at 2 pm. and was completed at 5 pm. The Battn marched to VILLE arriving in heavy rain & occupied old billets.	
VILLE.	3.	—	In billets. Reveille at 4 AM. The Battn marched off at 8 AM. through BUIRE HEILLY BONNAY to LA NEUVILLE and went into billets. Capt. MILNE proceeded on leave.	Loss
LA NEUVILLE	4.	—	do. The Battn Bathing.	
do.	5.	—	do. Practised the attack from trenches.	
do.	6.	—	do. Battn Drill 8am early morning parade. World lifting from 10am to 4 pm. Tactical exercise for Senior officers at 5.30 pm.	
do.	7.	—	do. Church parade 8.40 AM.	
do.	8.	—	do. C Coy left to go under Brigade instructors. The remainder of Battn. practising attack of trenches	9.B 6 sheets

WAR DIARY or INTELLIGENCE SUMMARY

Army Form C. 2118

10 YORKSHIRE REGT.   Sheet No. 2.

Place	Date	Hour	Summary of Events and Information	Remarks and references to Appendices
LA NEUVILLE	May 9	—	In billets. The Battn. was inspected in attack over trenches by the 4th Army Commander, GEN. Sir H. RAWLINSON and by the Divisional. Comd, MAJ. GEN. JACOBS.	
do.	10.	—	do. Battn drill. 6.30 to 8 AM. Route march in afternoon. MAJOR FOWLER returned from leave.	
do.	11.	—	do. Coy and Battn drill in morning. Route march in afternoon.	
do.	12.	—	do. No parades in morning. Battn cleaning billets & preparing for the move. The Battn moved off at 3. P.M. to go under canvas in a wood near BRAY K.18.d.8.6. We arrived at 8 P.M. and had a very wet night.	
K.18.d.8.6	13.	—	Under canvas. The Battn moved off at 7 A.M. to undertake anti-aircraft work at L.2.a.10.9. and worked till 4.30 P.M. got back to camp at 5.30 a wet day and still raining. Ground very wet.	
do.	14.	—	do. Wet and windy. The same as on the 13th.	
do.	15.	—	do. Still raining. The Battn went for work at 7 AM but returned at 10 AM owing to the wet. Remainder of day spent in digging drains all over Camp and pacifying tents. 2nd Lt. G.B. HORNBY rejoined the Battn for duty & was posted to C. Coy. Lt. H.L. HARLAND (attd) do. do. A Coy. 2nd Lt. C.H. PERKINS do. do. B Coy.	
do.	16.	—	do. Very fine day. Battn on work as on 13th inst.	

Army Form C. 2118

WAR DIARY
or
INTELLIGENCE SUMMARY
(Erase heading not required.)

Yorkshire Regt. Sheet No 3.

Instructions regarding War Diaries and Intelligence Summaries are contained in F. S. Regs., Part II. and the Staff Manual respectively. Title Pages will be prepared in manuscript.

Place	Date	Hour	Summary of Events and Information	Remarks and references to Appendices
K.18.d.8.6.	July 18.	—	Under Canvas, very fine day, work as on 13th.	
do.	19.	—	do.	
do.	20.	—	Lt. O.H. Ball rejoined the Battn. and was posted to D.Coy. work as on the 13th inst.	
do.	21.	—	do.	
do.	22.	—	Lt. Col. EDDOWES returned from leave. MAJOR. SHAND returned from FLEXICOURT. Capt. BARRACLOUGH do. leave. Capt. MILNE appointed temporary TOWN MAJOR of MEAULTE.	
do.	22.	—	do. The Battn paraded ready to move off by Platoons at 8.p.m. to billets in MEAULTE. The platoons moved off at 5 minutes interval. The relief of the 8th SOMERSET L.I. in the village was completed at 10.30.pm.	
MEAULTE	23.	—	In billets. All the Battn. were out on working parties up in the trenches. (work going on day and night) in different grades.	
do.	24.	—	do. work as on the 23rd.	
do.	25.	—	do.	

WAR DIARY
INTELLIGENCE SUMMARY

10 Yorkshire Regt.   Sheet No. 4.

Army Form C. 2118

Place	Date	Hour	Summary of Events and Information	Remarks and references to Appendices
MEAULTE.	May 26	—	In billets. work as usual about 2 p.m. the enemy put about 6 x 11 cm. shells into the middle of the village, near the Church, no damage was done. 18942 Pte. W. KING. (D) wounded on working party.	
do.	27	—	The Batt. paraded at 6.30 a.m. to relieve the 1st LINCOLNS, in the right section from THE CEMETERY (inclusive) to PURFLEET. The relief was completed at 10.30 A.M. Several large bombs were sent over about 11 A.M. The right section of trenches run from F.9.a.6.6½. to F.3.a.1.4. There was a considerable amount of shelling during the whole day. No. 11961. Pte. E. RAINSFORTH. (C) wounded. " 13074 " J. EVANS. (A) do. 2nd C.J. KINNACH rejoined the Batt. and resumed his Coy.	
Trenches.	28.	—	In night death handed, a large number of Rifle Grenades, Large Bombs & Shells were sent over by the enemy. one shell unfortunately burst in the fire trench & killed four men. Early in the A.M. it seemed as though the enemy were trying to find Batt. H.Q. as F.8. a. 3. but they were not successful. The enemy again in the evening sent more Bombs over, & caused more casualties	

WAR DIARY
or
INTELLIGENCE SUMMARY
(Erase heading not required.)

Yorkshire Regt. Sheet No. 5.

Army Form C. 2118

Place	Date	Hour	Summary of Events and Information	Remarks and references to Appendices
Trenches	Ap 28	—	No. 19466 Pt. J. BESTFORD. (C) Coy. Killed.	
			14139 Pt. H. COOPER. " 20347 Pt. D. BENNETT [W] (C) do. do.	
			19293 Sgt. W. CLEMMITT do. 18520 " T. THOMPSON (D) do. do.	
			13853 Pt. W. JAMESON do. 17488 " J.T. McGEE. (D) do. do.	
			20610 " A. PICKERSGILL (B) wounded 15137 " M. KENDALL (C) " wounded.	
			14703 " R. ROBSON do. 20334 " W. WALLACE (C) do.	
			15601 " J. E. WILD do. 17466 Sgt. A. G. TAYLOR (D) do.	
			8561 Cpl. J. THIRKILL do. 6914 " J. J. BYASS (D) do.	
			17415 Pt. A. FERGUSON do. 19423 Pt. J. H. DIXON (D) do.	
			17578 " A. M. WATSON do. 17469 " J. JOBSON (D) do.	
			14479 " R. LUMSDEN do. 11333 A.Cpl. H. SAMPSON (D) do.	
			do. 20532 Pt. C. MILNES. (D) do.	
			20307 L.Cpl. R. J. ELLIS. (A) Coy. wounded.	
do.	29.	—	On right sector of trenches, a much quieter day, and no casualties reported up to 8 p.m. a few rifle grenades & bombs were sent over by the enemy but were harmless, about 6.45, one of our heavy shells (9.2?) to pitch on a "delicate spot" in the enemy's lines, it brought forth immediate retaliation of about 15, 7.7 and 6, 15 cm. shells. by these fell harmlessly.	

WAR DIARY
or
INTELLIGENCE SUMMARY

(Erase heading not required.)

Army Form C. 2118

10 Yorkshire Regt.   Sheet No 6.

Place	Date	Hour	Summary of Events and Information	Remarks and references to Appendices
TRENCHES.	Aug 30	—	Our night sector of trenches, a fairly quiet night, until about 4.30.A.M. when the O/po [?] Divisional artillery made a combined bombardment of the enemy's defences. This brought only slight retaliation. Between 11.1.12 a.m. the enemy again tried to find B.H.Q. with 15 Cm. How: but were not successful, about 9 p.m. and later, the enemy sent a large number of aniseed and 15 cm shells into our trenches & supports, no serious casualties. 2nd Lieut. F.M.SHAW. (D) (by wounded) 10071 L.Cpl. S. PURKISS (A) do. 14185 Pri. M. MASON. (A) do. 15535 " T. PATTERSON. (A) do. 18991 " G. SMITHERS. (A) do.	
do.	31.	—	do. After canisters were sent over by the enemy but we replied in [?] otherwise our front was fairly quiet up till 1 mid-day [?] the afternoon passing through the night, several canisters came into our line & also some of a new type fell at about [?] caused some casualties. 10685 Pri. J.BENNETT. (D) wounded. 16414 L.Cpl. J.CROUDSON. (D) wounded. 17363 L.Cpl. J.W.BENNETT (D) do. 16362 Pri. W.DEARN (D) do. 17345 Pri. J.ARTHUR (A) do. 12169 L.Cpl. J.W.LAKENBY (B) do. 1503 " J.MATHER (B) do. 12128 Pri. F. MOONEY (B) do. 18424 " E.SELBY (A) do. 19575 Pri. J.TOGIVER (A) do. 14563 " J. SMITH (D) do. 18367 Pri. J.SUMMERSCALES (D) do.	

W.R.Williams
Lt.Col. Ret.
Commanding 10 Yorks. Regt.

Army Form C. 2118.

10 York Reg
vol 10

WAR DIARY
or
INTELLIGENCE SUMMARY
(Erase heading not required.)

10 Yorkshire Regt. Sheet No 1.

10.B.
Reg. books

Place	Date	Hour	Summary of Events and Information	Remarks and references to Appendices
Trenches	June 1.	—	In right sector a fairly quiet morning. The Battn were relieved by the 9th K.O.Y.L.I. The relief being completed about 12.30 p.m. The Battn marched back to BUIRE. two Coys being in billets and two in bivouac.	
BUIRE.	2.	—	The Battn paraded ready to move off at 8 A.M. to march to LA NEUVILLE, and arrived there at 11.30 A.M. and went into billets. The remainder of the day was spent in cleaning up and washing several men who had been suffering from "Shell Shock" rejoined the Battn.	
LA NEUVILLE.	3.	—	In billets the Battn cleaning and bathing.	
do.	4.	—	In billets the Battn were inspected at 10.30 AM by Brigadier General E.M. WILKINSON comdg. 62nd Inf. Bgd. and afterwards were dismissed for the day.	
do.	5.	—	Battn went march in morning. Company work in afternoon.	
do.	6.	—	do.	
do.	7.	—	morning as parade attry wet. Company work in afternoon.	
do.	8.	—	Inspection by Lieut General CAMPBELL comdg. 2nd Division after inspection the Battn were practised in the attack. Company work in afternoon. Battn Drill and Route March	
do.	9.	—	morning occupied by an attack in which communication with aeroplane was practised by the use of flares. afternoon bathing parade. 5.30 pm school interior Brigade sports.	
do.	10.	—	Route March in morning afternoon Brigade sports.	

Army Form C. 2118.

WAR DIARY
or
INTELLIGENCE SUMMARY
(Erase heading not required.)

10 Yorkshire Regt.   Sheet No. 2.

Place	Date	Hour	Summary of Events and Information	Remarks and references to Appendices
LA NEUVILLE	June 11	—	The Battn paraded ready to move off at 5.30 A.M. from LA NEUVILLE and moved to VILLE (one Coy). MEAULTE (two Coys) and the intermediary line (one Coy) to relieve the 4th MIDDLESEX Regt who had gone into trenches. Billets at the two villages were taken over at 11.30 A.M. and intermediary line about 2 P.M. Lt. Col. W.B. EDDOWES attending 4th ARMY SCHOOL at FLEXICOURT. Battn under command of MAJOR R.V. FOWLER. Battn H.Q. in MEAULTE.	
MEAULTE	12.	—	In billets. The Battn on working parties.	
do.	13.	—	do. A very wet day.	
do.	14.	—	do. All officers who could be spared and N.C.Os attended a lecture on "Bayonet fighting etc." at BUIRE.	
do.	15.	—	do.	
do.	16.	—	18638. Sgt. J. HALL (D) Coy wounded. 14354. S/M. A. BANNISTER (D) " do.	
do.	17.	—	Lt. Col. EDDOWES returned from FLEXICOURT. During the morning a shell fell in the street of MEAULTE as some horses were passing. One man killed, another wounded, and seven horses had to be killed. We had no casualties. A conference was held at 62nd Brigade H.Q. for C.O. at 4. p.m.	

WAR DIARY or INTELLIGENCE SUMMARY

Army Form C. 2118.

10 Yorkshire Regt.   Sheet No 3.

Place	Date	Hour	Summary of Events and Information	Remarks and references to Appendices
MEAULTE	June 18.	—	In Billets. The Battn. on working parties. 14515 S/Sgt. E.S. RIMER (GS) wounded whilst detonating bombs. 11333 L/Cpl. H. SAMPSON. do. do. 22848 Pte. J.H. KENDALL. do. do.	
do.	19.	—	The following officers reported for duty with the Battn. and were posted as under. NAME — Coy. posted to. Lieut. G.H.V. SAUNDERS ┐ L.I. COLLINS ├ to A. Coy. R.A.P. HARE ┘ 2nd Lt. F.P. CLIFF — to B. Coy. 2nd Lt. H.A. CORNABY ┐ A.E. GRIFFIN ├ to C. Coy. J.L. SMITH ┘ 2nd Lt. C.S. CARSON ┐ M. KEMP-WELCH ┘ to D. Coy.	
do.	20.	—	The Battn. relieved the 8th Somerset L.I. in Queens Redt. Bonte Redt. & Becordel. One Coy in each of the Redoubts (Cm Queens) (Bm Bonte) (A+D in Becordel) the relief proceeded. MEAULTE CHURCH at 9.30 A.M., and was completed at 12 noon. Battn. H.Q. in MEAULTE at E.17. 6.0.3. (1/20.000) Sheet 62 D.N.E. 13521 Pte. T. WADE (A) Coy. wounded (whole) 19642 ... W. BROWN (A) ... do. (whole) 6335 ... A. SUMNER (A) ... do.	

Army Form C. 2118.

WAR DIARY
or
INTELLIGENCE SUMMARY
(Erase heading not required.)

10 Yorkshire R.of. Sheet No 4.

Place	Date	Hour	Summary of Events and Information	Remarks and references to Appendices
REDOUBTS, #) BECORDEL	June 21	—	Battn in redoubts etc. The whole of BECORDEL (in our area) for working parties.	
do.	22	—	working parties as usual. A very quiet day. In MEAULTE (wounded on working parties) 11332 Pte. J. MARRIOTT. (B) (by wounded) 13917 " R. WILKINSON. C. do. 27496 " S. ARROWSMITH. A. do. 12288 " W.E. OAKLEY. B. do. 14363 L/Cpl. J.W. BENNETT. D. do. 14405 Pte. C. ELDRED. D. do.	
do.	23	—	do.	
do.	24	—	Battn. working on QUEEN'S ROI. and BRITTON ST. No places for us to assault. The underground system of trenches here viewed up during W. night. The [ref] night(?) bombardment [of 23+24] and the enemy bombarded them at 3.30 AM. Our intensive bombardment commenced at 6.30 AM. This bombardment go's on till X day. Then we attack. very little reply. 10 our force up to 1 p.m. during the afternoon tonight the enemy sent over some gas shells. but not to any great extent. 11361 Sgt. H. PIKE (B) (by wounded) 14138 Pte. F. KELD. D. do.	

Army Form C. 2118.

WAR DIARY
or
INTELLIGENCE SUMMARY
(Erase heading not required.)

Sheet No. 5.

10 Yorkshire Regt.

Place	Date	Hour	Summary of Events and Information	Remarks and references to Appendices
REDOUBTS etc.	June 25	—	V. day during the day and all night our bombardment was every in tensity, and searching the whole of the Enemy Position. as far as can be seen the retaliation by the enemy was on ALBERT. 7642 Sgt. T. WALTON. (a) (5) Wounded. 21006 A/Sgt. T. BILL. do.	
do.	26.	—	W. day the bombardment going on the whole time with heavy intensive during the morning both Gun & STOKES. GUNS were used, with good effect was hoped. the Enemy established in our front line trenches. 2nd A. G.H. MATHER reported for duty with the Battn two platoons to D. Coy. The III Corps. tried a Gas attack. commencing at 6 p.m. to the N of our trenches. 20265 Pt. R.R. THOMPSON (a) Coy Killed.	
do.	27.	—	X. day. bombardment still going strong more by gunfire than previously, the Battn moved from BOUZ. and BECORDEL. into QUEENS. Redbt in preparation for attack, all spare officers above the 25 Coy. into action returned to Q.M. stores at WILLE.	
QUEENS Redt.	28.	—	Y. day. intense bombardment a very wet day. we heard about 6 p.m. that the attack for Z. morning was postponed for 48 hours. the Battn were relieved by the 4th MIDDLESEX. Regt. relief completed about 11 p.m. and the Battn marched into billets in BUIRE.	

Army Form C. 2118.

WAR DIARY
or
INTELLIGENCE SUMMARY
(Erase heading not required.)

16 Yorkshire Regt.   Sheet No 6

Place	Date	Hour	Summary of Events and Information	Remarks and references to Appendices
BUIRE.	June 29	—	On billets. The battn cleaning and bathing.	
			12400 L/Cpl. W. RAMSDEN (C) Coy. Killed.	
			4989 " J.W. LACKENBY. C " wounded	
			2666 Pvt. T. NYLAND. C " do	
			4434 " FEATON. D " do	
			8546 " W. SIMPSON. D " do	
			18140 L/Cpl. C. LEVITT. C " do	
do.	30.	—	do. The Battn received telegram and ordered to Kit- The Battn. moved into QUEEN'S Redoubt leaving BUIRE. at 9.p.m. in readiness for attack which is to take place on morning of July 1. Q.M. stores moved to VILLE.	

W. Hallam
Lt. Col. Commanding, 16 Yorkshire Regt.

62nd Inf.Bde.
21st Div.

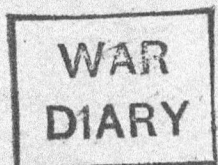

10th BATTN. THE YORKSHIRE REGIMENT.

J U L Y

1 9 1 6

Army Form C. 2118

WAR DIARY
or
INTELLIGENCE SUMMARY
(Erase heading not required.)

10 YORKSHIRE Regt. Sheet No. 1.

VOL 11

Place	Date	Hour	Summary of Events and Information	Remarks and references to Appendices
In the Field	1916 July 1. 2. 3.	-	Took part in the Battle of the SOMME. and got as far as CRUCIFIX TRENCH where we were relieved and marched back to DERNANCOURT into bivouac. (more detail cannot be given, owning to Col EDDOWES. being sent to England, sick, & having taken the fuller details with him. a special report has been already sent to the 21st Division)	
DERNANCOURT	4.	-	At DERNANCOURT. waiting for train. very heavy rain & no shelter for many every body wet through and no food. train arrived to come about 10 am. didn't arrive till about 6 pm. the 1 Battn entrained and arrived at AILLY sur SOMME about 11 pm and went into billets.	
AILLY S. Somme	5.	-	The Battn resting.	
do.	6.	-	do. and cleaning also Kit inspections etc. for re-fitting.	
do.	7.	-	The Battn moved from AILLY. s.s. at 9.30 AM and marched through. CAVILLON & OISSY to MOULIENS VIDAME. arriving there about 3 pm and went into billets a very wet march and men very wet.	
MOULIENS VIDAME	8.	-	On billets. The 62 Bgd. were inspected by M.G. General. CAMPBELL comdg. 21 Division. at 10 AM remainder of day resting.	
do.	9.	-	do. The Battn bathing by Coys. New & freer clothing etc. all handed to move at 2 pm.	

11.B. 6 sheets

WAR DIARY
or
INTELLIGENCE SUMMARY

(Erase heading not required.)

Army Form C. 2118

10 Yorkshire Regt. Sheet No 2

Place	Date	Hour	Summary of Events and Information	Remarks and references to Appendices
MOULLIENS VIDAME	July 10	—	Lt. Col. EDDOWES unfortunately went sick. The Command of the Battn being taken over by MAJOR V. FOWLER. The Battn left MOULLIENS VID. at 5.20 AM and marched to AILLY S.S. and entrained. The trains as usual being late. We detrained at CORBY, and then marched to MEAULTE, arriving there about 4 AM next morning (The 11th July) men worn out.	
MEAULTE	11	—	Trying to re-fit Battn. The 62nd Bgd receives orders to relieve a WELSH Bgd and finish the clearing of MAMETZ WOOD. The relief was not completed till about 4 AM and we carried out during very heavy shell fire on the wood.	
In the FIELD	12	—	In MAMETZ WOOD. Col. the wood quite clear and captured some guns busy consolidating. The Battn held the E. edge of the wood from N.E. corner to S. 20. a. 1.5. The enemy shelling was very heavy and caused many casualties including 2nd Lieut HORNSBY. Our bombardment then in preparation for attack on the 14th.	
MAMETZ WOOD	13	—	In wood, barrage during night G.12. x 13 very heavy also during afternoon. The troops to attack, assembled about 10.30 p.m. ready for assault on morning of 14th.	
do.	14	—	In wood, attack started at 3.25 am by 110 Bgd. and they took BEXANTINE LE PETIT wood (almost) and part of VILLAGE of same name. We were heavily shelled in MAMETZ WOOD.	

WAR DIARY or INTELLIGENCE SUMMARY

Army Form C. 2118

10 Yorkshire Regt.   Sheet No 3

Place	Date	Hour	Summary of Events and Information	Remarks and references to Appendices
MAMETZ WOOD.	July 15	—	In wood. Bombardment started again, and we had a number of our shells in our wood. The day was occupied in burying our own and German dead. About 9.30 p.m. the C.O. C. 62 Lt Regt. ordered the 10/6 Yorkshire Regt. to take a piece of road in front of BEZANTINE LE PETIT. WOOD. this piece of road could not to be taken by the 11th Bgd. H'd Qrs. (D.Y.C.) were sent forward under Capt CROWE and Capt COATER. The road was taken with only a few casualties and then handed over to the 110 Bgd. to consolidate unfortunately we lost Lieut CORMADY } both Killed. KINNACH }	
do.	16.	—	In wood. a fairly quiet day. swept for odd shells. busy cleaning up the wood etc. and strengthening our trenches and strong points.	
do.	17.	—	do. another fairly quiet day and further consolidation of trenches done. The Battn was relieved by the 9th HIGHLAND L.I. the relief being completed at 4.30 am. The Battn marched into billets in BUIRE. for a rest.	
BUIRE.	18.	—	In Billets. arrive here about 6.45 am. The Battn resting.	
do.	19	—	do. Battn re-fitting forming new L.G. Teams Battn Bombers etc. to be ready when we are wanted.	

Army Form C. 2118

WAR DIARY
or
INTELLIGENCE SUMMARY
(Erase heading not required.)

1st/6th Yorkshire Regt. Sheet No. 1

Place	Date	Hour	Summary of Events and Information	Remarks and references to Appendices
BUIRE	July 20.	—	Left BUIRE at 2.45 AM for DERNANCOURT entrained there at 6.40 AM (trains again late) arrived at SALEUX about 11. A.M. and then marched to MOULIENS VIDAME into billets as before. arrived there 5 pm. Transport arrived at 2 am on 21st.	
MOULIENS VID.	21.	—	In billets parades under Coy arrangements, re-fitting etc.	
do.	22.	—	do. Battn. had orders to move to RIFLE RANGE W of AMIENS. Left MOULIENS VIDAME in Busses at 4 pm and arrived on Ranges about 6.30 pm and went into bivouac there.	
RIFLE RANGES.	23.	—	Left Range at 6.18 am to entrain at LONGUEAU arrived at station at 8.20 am and entrained at once. Left LONGUEAU at 9.18. am (punctual for once) and arrived at PETIT HEUVIN about 2 pm. detrained and marched to TERNAS. into billets arriving there about 4 pm	
TERNAS	24.	—	In billets. Commenced Coy training and general re-organisation of Battn etc. received orders to move to MANIN. Left TERNAS at 5.30 pm. (advance of MANIN) about 4.40 pm. went into billets	
MANIN	25.	—	In billets Coy training etc. continued	

Army Form C. 2118

WAR DIARY
or
INTELLIGENCE SUMMARY
(Erase heading not required.)

10 Yorkshire Regt. Reel No 5.

Place	Date	Hour	Summary of Events and Information	Remarks and references to Appendices
MANIN	July 26.	—	In billets. Coy training etc. C.O. & O.C. Coys went to ARRAS. to inspect the section of line the Battn will take over.	
do.	27.	—	In billets. The Battn moved in busses at 10 A.M. to WANEQUETIN and stopped there till 8.30 p.m. then moved into billets in ARRAS, arriving there about 1. A.M. (28th) men but into underground passages, not fit for billets, road from WARLUS to ARRAS absolutely blocked with transport of all kinds. 2nd Lieut E. PEPPER (from 14th Battn) reported for duty, posted to D. Coy.	
ARRAS	28.	—	In billets. The Battn relieved the 6th K.O.Y.L.I. in trenches 88 to the bay N of JULY AV. and in BRITTANIA WORKS. B/e Battn left ARRAS at 3. p.m. and the relief was completed by 5.45 p.m. Battn H.Q. in SEPTEMBER AV. trenches 88 to 93 run from G. 14.b. 9½. 9 to G. 12.c. 3½. 9½. (map 57 B. N.W.3) 1/10,000.	
Trenches	29	—	In trenches 88-93 Battn in front & support line busy making dug outs for men. accommodation for men very bad. 2nd Lieut G. M. LAWLESS reported for duty. two p. platoons to C. Coy. do. B. Coy.	

2/Lt A. R. SLATER
p. A.D.S.S.

Army Form C. 2118

WAR DIARY
or
INTELLIGENCE SUMMARY
(Erase heading not required.)

10 Yorkshire Regt.   Sheet No 6.

Place	Date	Hour	Summary of Events and Information	Remarks and references to Appendices
TRENCHES	July 30	—	In trenches 88 to 93 and BRITTANIA WORKS. Battn repairing and revetting trenches, and getting dug outs sunk. a very quiet day. 2nd Lieut H.S. HARRISON (from 14 Battn) reported for duty, and was posted to D. Coy.	
do.	31	—	do. a quiet day. work on dug outs continued. 19165 Sgt. F.C. STUBBINGS. A Coy. wounded. 5281 Pte. W.W. ROBINSON. A " do. 5285 " F. SHEPHERD. B " do. (S*K*Y*L) (attached)	

V. Fowler. Major.
O.C. 10 Yorkshire Regt.

62nd Brigade.

21st Division.

1/10th BATTALION

YORKSHIRE REGIMENT

AUGUST 1916.

Army Form C. 2118.

VOL 12

WAR DIARY
or
INTELLIGENCE SUMMARY
(Erase heading not required.)

10 Yorkshire Regt.

Sheet No 1.

12.B.
6 sheets

Place	Date	Hour	Summary of Events and Information	Remarks and references to Appendices
Trenches	1916 Aug 1.	—	In trenches 88-93 & BRITTANIA WORK. Battn busy sinking oleff dug outs as on 31 July. will take about 3 weeks to complete. a very quiet day. Weather very hot.	
do.	2.	—	do. work on dug outs continued, a very quiet day.	
do.	3.	—	do. very quiet day. The Battn. was relieved by the 1st LINCOLN RGT. The relief being completed at 12.15 A.M. (4th). The Battn marched back to billets at AGNEZ-LEZ-DUISANS. arrived here 4 A.M.	
AGNEZ-LEZ DUISANS	4.	—	In billets at AGNEZ-LEZ-DUISANS. The Battn. resting; and Kits inspection in afternoon.	Han.
do.	5.	—	do. Coy training and training of bombers & other detachments. Battn talking by Bgd.	
do.	6.	—	do. Church Parade. visit of y LEICESTER REGT.	
do.	7.	—	do. Coy training and detachments also Battn at drilling.	
do.	8.	—	do. Coy training continued. recruit received & hisfinal. (CAMPBELL comdg. 21 Division)	

Army Form C. 2118.

WAR DIARY
or
INTELLIGENCE SUMMARY
(Erase heading not required.)

10 Yorkshire Regt.   Sheet No. 2.

Instructions regarding War Diaries and Intelligence Summaries are contained in F. S. Regs., Part II. and the Staff Manual respectively. Title Pages will be prepared in manuscript.

Place	Date	Hour	Summary of Events and Information	Remarks and references to Appendices
AGNEZ-LEZ-DUISANS.	Aug 9.	—	In billets at AGNEZ. The Battn relieved the 1st LINCOLN. REGT. in trenches 88-93 and BRITTANIA WORKS. Head of Battn left DAINEVILLE RAILWAY BRG at 9.p.m. relief was complete at 12.30 A.M. (10th).	
Trenches.	10.	—	In trenches 88-93 and BRIT. WK. a quiet day, deep dug outs and revetting being carried on.	
do.	11	—	do. 30/14944. Pte G. USHER. (C.S.) Killed. a quiet day. Work being continued, also in GORDON LINE. Trenches inspected by GENERAL HALDAIN, Lieut. GEN. CAMPBELL and BRIG. GEN. RAWLING. MAJOR FOWLER sent to hospital. Command of Battn taken over by Capt. BARRACLOUGH.	
do.	12.	—	do. a very quiet day. Work progressing satisfactorily.	
do.	13.	—	do. rather more activity on the Enemy's part with his trench mortars fortunately not on our Battn front. Work carried on as usual making good progress with dug outs & in support line	

WAR DIARY
or
INTELLIGENCE SUMMARY

Army Form C. 2118

10 Yorkshire Regt.   Sheet No 3.

Place	Date	Hour	Summary of Events and Information	Remarks and references to Appendices
Trenches	Aug 14.	—	In trenches 88-93. and BRIT. WK. a few shells fell in the Battn area, b.t did no damage, otherwise quiet, at about 10 P.M. the enemy exploded a mine in the area held by the Battn on our Left. (110 BGD). No action followed. No damage was done to trenches in our Battn sector. No 5284. Pte. ROSENBLUM. T. (AG) wounded.	
do.	15.	—	a very quiet day. work proceeding as usual.	
do.	16.	—	There seemed to be a good deal of ARTILLERY work in H sector, nothing reported on our front. very quiet.	
do.	17.	—	Brigadier GEN. RAWLING inspected trenches and work completed. The best Bay considered being No1 Bay in BRIT work occupied by B. Coy. a quiet day. and work progressing well.	
do.	18.	—	The Battn was relieved in trenches by 9th LEICESTER. RGT. commencing at 12.30 p.m. on being relieved the Battn then proceeded to débus at bottom of M. [?] from S. R. SCARP. (C.Cy. to ST SAUEUR. WKS relieving 6th K.E. YORKS. A. Coy. to CEMETERY. WKS relieving S. STAFFORD. RGT. HQ. and B + D Coy. filling in 1 LINCOLN RGT Billets in ARRAS. relief completed at 3.30 p.m. Lieut. LONEY. proceeded on Special leave	

Army Form C. 2118

WAR DIARY
or
INTELLIGENCE SUMMARY
(Erase heading not required.)

10 Yorkshire Regt.   Sheet No. 7,

Instructions regarding War Diaries and Intelligence Summaries are contained in F. S. Regs., Part II. and the Staff Manual respectively. Title Pages will be prepared in manuscript.

Place	Date	Hour	Summary of Events and Information	Remarks and references to Appendices
ARRAS.	Aug 19.	—	In billets in ARRAS. 12 6p.m. works. very quiet day. Working parties provided by Coys in ARRAS.	
do.	20.	—	MAJOR FOWLER returned from hospital & took over comd of the Battn.	
do.	21.	—	a quiet day. working parties as usual.	
			do.	
			do.	
			CEMETERY WORKS situated in G.23.d. and G.29.b. G.29.d. St. SAVEUR. Map Ref. ARRAS 51B N.W.3. 1/10,000	
do.	22.	—	a quiet day. working parties provided. Garrisons of works busy tapping sumps in Comn. trenches & putting fire Bays in order. Inspection of billets in ARRAS.	
do.	23.	—	do.	
do.	24.	—	do.	
do.	25.	—	a quiet day. working parties as usual.	

Army Form C. 2118

WAR DIARY
or
INTELLIGENCE SUMMARY
(Erase heading not required.)

10 Yorkshire Regt.   Sheet No. 5

Place	Date	Hour	Summary of Events and Information	Remarks and references to Appendices
ARRAS	Aug 26.	—	Disposition came noon 25th. The Battn. relieved 1st LINCOLN Regt. in I.2 sector. Comprising trenches 61 to 72 inclusive. The relief was completed by 6.15 pm. Trenches 61-72. extend from G.30.a.7½.5. to G.24.a.2.8. (The R. SCARP) Map Ref. ARRAS. 51B. N.W. 3. 1/10,000.	
Trenches.	27.	—	In trenches 61-72. A very quiet night. Also day. Battn. working at revetting; and draining Comm. trenches by sumps, and placing "Duck Boards" down.	
do.	28.	—	do. Very quiet all the time. Work on trenches being continued.	
do.	29.	—	do. A very quiet day on our own sector, but on night of I. sector there was a raid by 60th Division, as far as could be seen (heard) there was very little opposition to raid by German artillery. About midnight we sent about 30 rifle grenades into German works. Got very slight retaliation in reply. He used our "STOKES" GUN. no reply.	
do.	30.	—	do. A very quiet day and night. Had very heavy rain storms. Work on trenches continued, trenches getting rather wet	

1875 Wt. W593/826 1,000,000 4/15 J.B.C. & A. A.D.S.S./Forms/C. 2118.

Army Form C. 2118

WAR DIARY
or
INTELLIGENCE SUMMARY
(Erase heading not required.)

10 Yorkshire Regt.   Sheet No. 6.

Place	Date	Hour	Summary of Events and Information	Remarks and references to Appendices
TRENCHES.	Aug 3/14	—	On trenches 61 to 72 inclusive, a quiet day and night on our sector front. A raid took place by the Enemy on our trenches N. of R. SCARP. Result not known. 1st enfo[5]3 STOKES. GUN. and 2" MORTAR several times during day on left. Lieut F.B. PARKER reported for duty, posted to D Co. 2 Lieut T.R. EVANS. do to A Co. 70/20/0 Pte. C.F. BARR. (C Co.) wounded 19580 Pte. J. HEPPLE (A Co.) wounded. 5234 " C Cox (C Co.) do } from S.y + S. mortar attacks	

J. Fowler, Lt Col
Commanding 10 Yorkshire Regt.

62nd Brigade.

21st Division.

1/10th BATTALION

YORKSHIRE REGIMENT

SEPTEMBER 1916.

Army Form C. 2118.

WAR DIARY
or
INTELLIGENCE SUMMARY
(Erase heading not required.)

Instructions regarding War Diaries and Intelligence Summaries are contained in F.S. Regs., Part II. and the Staff Manual respectively. Title Pages will be prepared in manuscript.

10, Yorkshire Rgt.

62/57 Rec. No. 1, vol. 13

13. B. 6 sheet

Place	Date	Hour	Summary of Events and Information	Remarks and references to Appendices
In Trenches	Sept 1.	—	In trenches 61-72. day very quiet, work as usual carried on. The Battn. was relieved by the 1st. Lincoln Rgt. The relief being completed by 12.30 A.M. on the 2nd. The Battn. marched to billets at DANEVILLE, arriving there about 1.30 A.M. 2nd Lt. UZZELL wounded.	
DANEVILLE.	2.	—	In billets. The Battn. proceeded by route Buses to SOMBRIN. in 6 billets. arriving about 2.30 A.M. 3/9/16. Capt. G.A. TURNER rejoined the Battn. for duty.	
SOMBRIN.	3.	—	In billets. The Battn. cleaning up etc. The M.O. proceeded to 69 F.A. for a course of instruction. Lt. MATTHEWS took over duties of Battn. M.O.	
do.	4.	—	Work as per programme. Coy training.	
do.	5.	—	Coy training and re-filling. 2nd Lt. DICKINSON returned from leave. Capt. W. COATER returned from 3rd Army school and took over command of A.C.B. from 2nd Lt. SLATER.	oaks
do.	6.	—	Coy training per special programme. Lt. Col. V. FOWLER returned from leave & took over command	

Army Form C. 2118.

WAR DIARY
or
INTELLIGENCE SUMMARY
(Erase heading not required.)

10 Yorkshire Regt. Sheet No 2

Place	Date	Hour	Summary of Events and Information	Remarks and references to Appendices
SOMBRIN.	Sept. 7.	—	In billets. Brigade road march in morning. Coy training in afternoon.	
do.	8.	—	Morning Coy lecture & practice Advance guard etc. afternoon conference at Brigade H.Q. at 4.30 p.m. and lecture to officers from 6.30 to 7 p.m.	
do.	9.	—	Company training and re-fitting.	
do.	10.	—	The Battn. were addressed by Major Gen. CAMPBELL commdg. 21. Divn. Church parade afternoon. Coy training	
do.	11.	—	Battn. training on training area. Outposts. Battn up to strength, first time since battle of LOOS.	
do.	12.	—	The Battn moved out of village at 3.30 p.m. marching to REBREUVIETTE. arriving at 6. p.m. very few billets. two Coys having to bivouac.	
do. etc.	13.	—	Thus at 6 A.M. the Battn moved off. and marched to FREVENT entraining there at 8.28. a.m. arrived at ALBERT. about 10. P.M. (train about 9 hours late) marched to bivouacs about half way between ALBERT and DERNANCOURT. ground very wet.	
REBREUVIETTE.	13.	—		

Army Form C. 2118.

WAR DIARY
or
INTELLIGENCE SUMMARY

(Erase heading not required.)

10th Yorkshire Regt.

Place	Date	Hour	Summary of Events and Information	Remarks and references to Appendices
Bivouac	Sept/14	—	In bivouac getting camp into order, inspection of arms, returns, gas helmets etc. Bivouac at E.9.c. central.	Sheet 57 c 3
do.	15th	—	Left bivouac at 2 a.m. and moved to BECORDEL CAMP (E.12.9. central) arrived there at 10 a.m. refitting remainder of day.	
do.	16th	—	Left BECORDEL CAMP at 6 a.m. arrived at POMMIERS REDT. and MONTAUBAN at 9 a.m. Left redoubt at 9 p.m. to relieve trenches near GUEUDECOURT. Relief complete at 6.45 a.m. (on 17th) trenches situated N.31.b.4.0. to N.31.b.4.0. Sheet 57 c SW.	
Trenches	17th	—	In front line, considerable shelling on both sides, in touch on left flank with QUEENS W. SURREY on right flank with 13. N.F. busy consolidating. There was an attack by Brigade on our right on BIRD TRENCH.	
do.	18th	—	Rained very wet. 6 in. to 2 ft. of mud and slush. the usual bombardment going on the whole time, men very wet and uncomfortable. Issue of Rum a blessing, in early morning to them, food & water coming up very steadily, owing to bad state of roads etc.	

WAR DIARY / INTELLIGENCE SUMMARY

Army Form C. 2118.

Yorkshire Regt. Sheet No 4.

Place	Date	Hour	Summary of Events and Information	Remarks and references to Appendices
TRENCHES	1916 Sept 19.	—	On front line; usual shelling going on; many wounded. The usual shelling going on. The troops we relieved were terribly ill, got away. They belonging to the troops we relieved, and the inability to difficulty we had to get R.A.M.C. help to get them away. The work at N.33.a. central was occupied and consolidated at N.E. corner. D. Co. being the Co. to find the party under Lieut PARKER.	
do.	20."	—	1. LINCOLNS made a bombing attack on point 91. (N.33.d.9.1.) most very successful. artillery very active on both sides, had to make serious complaint about our Heavies dropping shells in our own front line trenches and causing casualties, very bad shooting. The usual shooting happened every day.	
do.	21."	—	A quiet night compared with others. 14. N.F. dug a trench from N.33.d.7.3 to N.33.a. central, which we patrolled all night. The enemy shelling on our front line very heavy.	
do.	22.	—	Days amount of shelling on our front line & supports. The Batt. was relieved by 1st D.L.I. relief complete at 11.05 pm The Battn marched back to FRICOURT Camp. (F. 13. a. central)	

Army Form C. 2118.

WAR DIARY
or
INTELLIGENCE SUMMARY
(Erase heading not required.)

10 Yorkshire Regt. Sheet No 5.

Place	Date 1916	Hour	Summary of Events and Information	Remarks and references to Appendices
Bivouac.	Sept. 23.	—	In bivouac at FRICOURT CAMP. Men cleaning and resting.	
do.	24th	—	do. Church parade. Baths cleaning & re-fitting.	
do.	25th	—	Left FRICOURT CAMP. and moved to bivouac at S.22.d.4.5. waiting to go forward. attack time for 12.30 p.m.	
do.	26th	—	In bivouac at S.22.d.7.5. By parade etc. issue of bombs, etc. in readiness to move at one hours notice. Relieved the 6th Bgd. in front line, relief was complete at 4.45 am (6th D.) relieved the 13th N.F. and 10th K.O.Y.L.I.	
Trenches.	27	—	In trenches very busy consolidating; trenches mm from N.24.d.2.3. to N.24.c.5.9. considerable enemy shelling as we marched up to trenches we had a very unfortunate hostile accident which wounded 8 men, 2 Batln. Bombers. The enemy placed a very heavy barrage behind our support line brought on account of attack by Division on our left. (moved) Battn. H.Q. to N.33.a.2.7. 1/2. armies there at 4 p.m. and found a stranded "Tank" about 100yds away."	

2449 Wt. W14957/Mgo 750,000 1/16 J.B.C. & A. Forms/C.2118/12.

Army Form C. 2118.

WAR DIARY
or
INTELLIGENCE SUMMARY

(Erase heading not required.)

Yorkshire Regt. Part No. 6.

Place	Date	Hour	Summary of Events and Information	Remarks and references to Appendices
TRENCHES	Sept. 28	—	In trenches. A fairly quiet night consolidating hard, & our shells coming over all the time, about 8pm rather heavy shelling by port line & dugouts. Casualty Casualties:- Capt. W.R. KNOTT wounded. 2nd Lt. O.H. BELL Killed.	
do.	29	—	do. Another fairly quiet night, good digging done through night, also through day, which was very trying & tiring, during the day the enemy put over bursts of shells. An attempt was made to remove "tanks" but it was quite unsuccessful. The Batt. was relieved by the 1st D.C.L.I. relief was completed at 9.30 p.m. the Battn marched into Bivouac at L.16.d - S.22.a	
BIVOUAC	30	—	In Bivouac, as above, the Batt resting and cleaning up &c. inspections &c.	

J. Mowbray, Lt. Col.
Comg. 10 Yorkshire Regt.

Army Form C. 2118

Vol 14

WAR DIARY
or
INTELLIGENCE SUMMARY
(Erase heading not required.)

10 Yorkshire Regt. Sheet No 1.

Place	Date	Hour	Summary of Events and Information	Remarks and references to Appendices
In the FIELD.	1916. Oct.1	—	Left Bivouac at 8 A.M. and marched to BUIRE. Went under canvas, a very trying march for the men, their feet being soft, arrived at BUIRE about 2.6. p.m.	
BUIRE	2.	—	At BUIRE. under canvas, a very wet day, could do little in the way of work or cleaning up.	
do.	3.	—	very wet day. Left BUIRE at 3 p.m. for DERNANCOURT entrained at 4 p.m. (train left at 4 p.m.) detrained at LONGPRÉ about 2.30. a.m.(4th) marched to VILLIERS. SUR. AILLY. arrived about 5 p.m and went into Billets.	
VILLIERS. SUR.AILLY.	4.	—	At VILLIERS. men resting and cleaning up.	
do.	5.	—	do. Dry training and Bath dull. The clothing etc indented had not arrived. So no re-fitting could be done.	
do.	6.	—	do. Coy and Batt'n training. clothing (not yet arrived) was warned to go to Ordnance for it, about 36 hours late.	

1H.B
7 Minute

WAR DIARY
or
INTELLIGENCE SUMMARY

Army Form C. 2118

10 Yorkshire Regt — Sheet No 2

Place	Date	Hour	Summary of Events and Information	Remarks and references to Appendices
VILLIERS. Bog. Aux	Oct 7th	—	At VILLIERS. Coy training. Battn Bombers training at trenches near L'ETOILE.	
do.	8.	—	do. The Battn moved off at 4.30.A.M. to entrain at LONGPRÉ at 4.30am (for new area. train started about 10.A.M. (Late as usual) arrived at FOUQUEREUIL at 4.30 pm. (ought to have been there about 12.30 p.m.) marched to MARLES. LEZ. MINES into billets arriving there about 10·45 p.m.	
MARLES. LEZ. MINES.	9.	—	at MARLES. L. MINES. morning Battn resting. afternoon. Coy training under Coy arrangements.	
do.	10.	—	do. C.O. and ADJT. went by Bus at 8.A.M. to view new trenches. Battn moved to FOUQUEREUIL. Left MARLES. L.M. at 2.30. p.m. arrived at Billets at FOUQUEREUIL at 4.15 pm	
FOUQUER. EUIL	11.	—	At FOUQUEREUIL. Battn moved off at 12. noon. and marched into trenches in reserve, about our 6 miles march. The Battn relieved the 1st WORCESTER. REGT in CURLY. CRES. and O.B. LINES. relief was complete at 4.30. p.m.	

Army Form C. 2118

WAR DIARY
or
INTELLIGENCE SUMMARY
(Erase heading not required.)

Yorkshire Regt. Sheet No 3

Instructions regarding War Diaries and Intelligence Summaries are contained in F.S. Regs., Part II. and the Staff Manual respectively. Title Pages will be prepared in manuscript.

Place	Date	Hour	Summary of Events and Information	Remarks and references to Appendices
TRENCHES	Oct 12	—	IN RESERVE trenches. Situated about O.B.5. (C.11.C.20.05 to C.10.d.65.90) Trenches in a very bad state of repair, and dug out accommodation very bad. Hard work to get them into order. Battn busy making dug outs for cover, & extra on new ones.	
do.	13.	—	Very quiet, although work to be carried on during day light. No enemy shelling. Men still busy, and likely to be on dug outs etc	
do.	14.	—	Very quiet and usual work on repairs, new Dug outs being carried out.	
do.	15.	—	do.	
do.	16.	—	do.	
do.	17.	—	Rebuilding etc carried on. The 140 Inf. Brigade sector was altered. A&C Coy, 10 York & Lancs. Rn. thrown into Billets at NOYELLES, being relieved by 12 N.F. B Coy 10 Y&L took over while D. O.B.5 and CURLY CRES was occupied by D Coy 10 Y&L. Bombers & H.Q. D. 10 York Regt.	

1875 Wt. W5091/826 1,000,000 4/15 J.B.C. & A. A.D.S.S./Forms/C. 2118.

Army Form C. 2118

WAR DIARY
or
INTELLIGENCE SUMMARY
(Erase heading not required.)

10 Yorkshire Regt. Sheet No 4.

Place	Date	Hour	Summary of Events and Information	Remarks and references to Appendices
TRENCHES	Oct. 18	—	In Reserve trenches, rebuilding O.B.5. runs from G.11.C.20.05 to G.10.d.65.90 CURLY CUES.	
do.	19.	—	do. G.16.b.45.90 to G.10.d.45.85 +NOEUELLES. A very wet day and little work could be done. Trenches fell in several places. The result of no work having been done on them for some considerable time.	
do.	20.	—	day fine. Repair & clearing going on.	
do.	21.	—	The Battn relieved the 1st LINCOLN RGT in front line trenches from 94 to 106. taking in the QUARRY sector & part of the HOHENZOLLERN Redt. The trenches run from G.11.b.8½.3/6. G.4.d.10.1/2. The relief was completed at 4.50 pm.	
do.	22.	—	In trenches 94 – 106. fine weather before work carried out. Enemy quiet in morning. About 4.30 pm. two heavy "MINNENWERFER" fell in NORTHERN CRATER. and cause several casualties & considerable damage to defences.	

33147 P.I.T.AVIS. (B) Killed.   16492 L/Cp R.OTTERSON (3) WOUNDED 36368 Pte W.SYKES (B) wounded
36388 " A.F.SEDMAN (B) do.   15763 Pte J.W.BRIGHAM (B) do.   36302 " G.W.CURR (B) do.
36139 " F.COWLEY (B) do.   36147 " R.CARTER (B) do.   33065 " F.BONE (B) do. S.S
                                36147 " J.CONNELLY (B) do.   33145 " R.SPINKS (B) do. S.S
                                24614 " G.EVANS (B) do.   33125 " W.BRACEY (B) do. S.S
                                3/4113 " J.W.GRAY (B) do.   36125 " H.SYKES (B) do. S.S

WAR DIARY or **INTELLIGENCE SUMMARY**

Army Form C. 2118

10 Yorkshire Regt — Sheet No 5

Place	Date	Hour	Summary of Events and Information	Remarks and references to Appendices
Trenches	Oct 23	—	In trenches 94–106. A quiet day, no shelling and work going on satisfactorily. Trenches in a very bad and wet condition and trouble being up to the knees in places, and Gum Boots are a very bad for men's feet, owing to time in water, which takes the felt.	
do.	24	—	do. A quiet day. Trenches getting worse, and very wet day.	
do.	25	—	do. As usual a quiet day. The usual quantity of "Rum Jars" from the enemy, and DARTS. No casualties.	
do.	26	—	do. A quiet day. Draft of 12 men arrived. All hotter working parties concentrated on wiring during the night. 9481 Sgt C. KAY (@ wounded). 20360 Pte. S. SOTTERFIELD (C) do. 21620 " E. KERSHAW (C) do.	
do.	27	—	do. A quiet day on the whole. In afternoon enemy started "Rum Jars" came down, causing casualties. [?] the working party also had casualties. 15025 Pte TM.ELCH (A) Killed 33268 Pte. A. FRY (C) wounded 15888 L.Cpl. R.C. HOTCHINSON (A) do. 35212 " J.G. NESBITT do. 36362 Pte. F. HEPPER (D) do. 11403 " A. RICHARDSON (A) do.	

WAR DIARY
or
INTELLIGENCE SUMMARY

Army Form C. 2118

7th Yorkshire Regt.   Sheet No 6.

Place	Date	Hour	Summary of Events and Information	Remarks and references to Appendices
TRENCHES	Oct. 28th	—	On trenches 94-106. Repair work for posts and at night wiring during the night of 27th/28th. A quantity of "Rum Jars" came over between FRONT LINE and SUPPORTS. also during the afternoon of the 28th. Dispositions made to resist expected raid by enemy which did not come off. The "Run Jar" blew in a dug-out causing casualties: 12349 A. Cpl. D. BAINBRIDGE (2). killed. 33004 Pte. C.F.C. HEEVERS. (D). do. 29005 " A. WILSON (D). wounded. 36365 " E. HURLEY. (D). do. 33149 L.Cpl. E.B. RICHES. (D). do. S.S.	
do.	29th	—	Repair work carried on as usual day except for a few "Rum Jars" from the enemy. 26647 Pte. E. COOK. (D) killed.	

Army Form C. 2118

WAR DIARY
or
INTELLIGENCE SUMMARY

(Erase heading not required.)

10 Yorkshire Regt Sheet No 1

Place	Date	Hour	Summary of Events and Information	Remarks and references to Appendices
TRENCHES	1916 30	—	In trenches 94-106. a quiet day. The Battn. was relieved by the 2/Lincoln Rgt. in the front line, relief being completed at 12 noon, on relief the Battn. moved into the Support line to relieve the 2/R.F. which had already been relocated Support line runs from LE ROUTOIR ALLEY — along DEVON LANE — O.G.I. to CHAPEL ALLEY. — O.131. to GORDON ALLEY. No. up. C. from C.18.a.8.8. to C.10.6.9.1. 2nd in Command Rt. M. Mallory D. Kubba	
"	31st	—	In Support trenches as above, work on repair of trenches carried on, and working parties supplied to R.E. and Pioneers. (1/4 N.F.) a quiet day	

I Toulmin Lt Col
Commanding 10 Yorkshire Regt

Army Form C. 2118

WAR DIARY
or
INTELLIGENCE SUMMARY
(Erase heading not required.)

7o YORKSHIRE REGT. Sheet No V.P. 15

15.B.
6 sheets

Place	Date	Hour	Summary of Events and Information	Remarks and references to Appendices
TRENCHES.	1916 Nov. 1	—	In Support Trenches. a quiet day. work carried on in Communication Trenches, and working parties provided.	
do.	2.	—	a quiet day, rather wet. working parties as usual, and special party sent to keep HULLUCH and GORDON ALLEYES clean.	
do.	3.	—	still very quiet. work going on as usual. the trenches sliding in quicker than we can cope with it.	
do.	4.	—	a quiet day. work as usual.	
do.	5.	—	do a fine day but with heavy falls in trenches.	
do.	6.	—	a wet day. at 2.47 AM a patrol went out under S/ RAY. to try and establish the identity of the enemy on our front. he was not successful, finding two parties of the enemy waiting for him.	
do.	7.	—	The Battn relieved the 1st LINCOLN RGT. in the front line in trench 74–106. relief was complete by 1. P.M. a very wet day, and trenches getting much worse.	Ly4

Army Form C. 2118

WAR DIARY
INTELLIGENCE SUMMARY
(Erase heading not required.)

1/6 YORKSHIRE Regt.   Sheet No. 2

Place	Date	Hour	Summary of Events and Information	Remarks and references to Appendices
TRENCHES	2018.	—	In Trenches 94-106. A fairly quiet day. Trenches in a very bad condition, falling in all over. Worse than we can put them up again. 33/44 Pte. T. CORBYN (C) Killed. 26616 Cpl. BROADBENT (D) wounded. 36326 Pte. A. SHAW. (B) do.	
do.	9.	—	do. A quiet day and fine. Busy digging a way through trenches which have fallen in. Front line very bad. Also communication trenches up to it.	
do.	10.	—	do. A fairly quiet day. The usual trench mortar work on both sides. A good drying day and repair work could be done well. Still a lot of water in the trenches. 33064 Pte. A. MATHER (B) wounded 19626 " J. HEATON (B) do. 26629 " A. DRUCE. (B) do.	
do.	11.	—	do. A quiet day. Very little trench mortar work by the enemy. Our usual quantity was sent over. Repair work going forward. Trenches getting a little dryer.	

WAR DIARY
or
INTELLIGENCE SUMMARY

Yorkshire Regt. Sheet No 3

Place	Date	Hour	Summary of Events and Information	Remarks and references to Appendices
Trenches	Nov 12	—	In trenches 94-106, enemy T.M. more active, repair work going on well, a fine day.	
			33091 Pt F.J. SLANEY (B) Killed.	
			13408 " J. GARDEN (C) wounded	
			36337 " W.L. BOWS 6/14 (C) do.	
			36126 " A. CARR. (B) do. S.S.	
do.	13.	—	usual repair work carried on, enemy T.M. rather busy, they were suitably replied to.	
do.	14.	—	26153. Cpl W. TANFIELD (C) wounded working parties on repair work, more activity on both sides with guns and a quantity of T.M. work.	
do.	15.	—	The Battn was relieved by 1st LINCOLN Regt relief being complete by 12.15 p.m. on relief the Battn went into reserve, two Coys (B&D) at NOVELLES, and 2 Coys (A+C) in CURLY CRES and O.B. 4 and S.	
do.	16	—	In Reserve. Coys in NOVELLES bathing and cleaning, other two Coys supplied working parties.	
do.	17	—	Coys in NOVELLES fitting new hot respirators, remainder of Battn supplied working parties.	

Army Form C. 2118

WAR DIARY
or
INTELLIGENCE SUMMARY
(Erase heading not required.)

10 YORKSHIRE Regt. Sheet No. 4.

Place	Date	Hour	Summary of Events and Information	Remarks and references to Appendices
TRENCHES	Nov. 18.	—	In Reserve. Inspection of Billets and men by C.O. rain commenced again making things very wet.	
do.	19.	—	wet day again. relief of R. Battn. from 110 Bgd. was appointed acting R. Col. and took over command of the Battn this day. MAJOR R. MATHIAS from 110 Bgd. was appointed acting R. Col. and took over command of the Battn this day.	
do.	20.	—	The Coys in NOVELLES relieving them. A.T.C. Coy went back to NOVELLES a quiet day, working parties as usual.	
do.	21.	—	weather finer. Coy in NOVELLES cleaning & bathing, working parties supplies by remainder of Battn. still fine. Coy in NOVELLES filling new hot ??? remainder at working parties as usual.	
do.	22.	—	The Battn relieved the 1st LINCOLN Regt. in front line taking over trenches 94 - 106 relief complete by 12.30 pm	
do.	23.	—	In trenches 94 - 106 a quiet day and good repair on trenches carried on. weather also fine.	

WAR DIARY
or
INTELLIGENCE SUMMARY

Army Form C. 2118

Sheet No. 5.

Yorkshire Regt.

Place	Date	Hour	Summary of Events and Information	Remarks and references to Appendices
TRENCHES.	Nov 24.	—	In trenches 94 – 106. Very heavy T.M. by the enemy on HOLLUCH ALLEY which was blown in badly. GORDON ALLEY also damaged. All precaution taken however any raid that might be made by the enemy. Instead of a busy night, everything on our front was more than ordinarily quiet, the enemy being rather nervous apparently, judged by the number of VERY lights they sent up.	
do.	25.	—	A fairly quiet day, rather damp and wet. We sent over the usual daily "Ration" of STOKES etc. In the afternoon a quantity of enemy T.M. came over.	

```
         33128  Pte  C. PEARSON     (A) killed   24.11.16
         26399   "   W. MORGAN      (C)  "          "
         24341   "   J. LUND        (C) wounded 16.11.16
         33122   "   S.H. BIGHAM    (C)  do       do.    S.S.
         24648   "   W.E. VERITY    (A)  do    24.11.16
              "       T.M. (enemy)  (A)  do        do
    in the enemy a T.M. (enemy) unfortunately turned some men.
   25300  L/Cpl  A. STAMP   (B) killed 22901 Cpl G.H. WILLIAMS (B) wounded
   33177   do    H.W. Fox   (B)   do   33198 L/Cpl R.W. PEART.  (B)   do
   19214  Pvt.   J. BURNIE  (D)   do   19156 Pvt.  J.P. BAWAI  (B)   do
                                 18164      "    J.M. FOSTER  (A)   do
```

WAR DIARY

Army Form C. 2118

10 YORKSHIRE Regt. Sheet No 6.

Place	Date	Hour	Summary of Events and Information	Remarks and references to Appendices
TRENCHES	Nov 26	—	In trenches 94 - 106. a quiet night and work going on satisfactorily. The usual quantity of T.M. came over, and further damage done to HULLUCH AND GORDON trenches. 25236 Pvt H. DWYER (D) wounded.	
do.	27	—	do. There was a bombardment by us of the enemy back areas etc which did not bring much retaliation, a few shells fell near VERMELLES	
do.	28	—	do. 19218 Cpl. R. CLARKE (D) wounded. a quiet night. The Batn. was relieved by 1st Lincoln Regt. relief complete at P. 45 p.m. The Batt. then relieved the 13th W.F. in support line. a quiet day.	
do.	29	—	In Support trenches. a very quiet night. also day. working parties provided 14313. Pvt. T.P. HOLIDAY (S) wounded 28.11.16.	
do.	30	—	do. a very quiet night and day. usual working parties provided	

T.A. Matthews Lt. Col.
Commanding 10 Yorks Regt.

Army Form C. 2118.

WAR DIARY
or
INTELLIGENCE SUMMARY
(Erase heading not required.)

10/YORKSHIRE REGT   Sheet No 1.   Vol 16

16.B.
6 sheets

Place	Date	Hour	Summary of Events and Information	Remarks and references to Appendices
TRENCHES	DEC 1.	—	In Seppet trenches, a quiet day, very cold and fairly dry. Batt. Bathing and working parties.	
do.	2.	—	do. a quiet day. Still very freezing cold but dry. Bathing & working parties.	
do.	3.	—	do. working parties as usual.	
do.	4.	—	do. The Batt. relieved the 1st LINCOLN REGT. in front line trenches 94-106. relief was complete at 11.30 am. a few 5.9 cm fell near EXETER CASTLE H.Q. but did no damage.	
do.	5.	—	In trenches 94-106. The enemy T.M.s were rather active and were in turn replied to by our own T.M. and STOKES. a dull day, in Loomre rain almost. The line was held on a new plan, 1 short platoon in each, with one platoon in each bat. the trenches between the bat. being patrolled by day & night and a crash attack is (S) here ard if located. STANCFIELD RD. & HE Trenches amounted to so so many a quiet day and work unk on trenches was also in progress.	
do.	6.	—	The forward W.E. temporary Rd. on STANDFIELD RD. for Coy HQ attack & Coy HQ was made cold.	

Army Form C. 2118.

WAR DIARY
or
INTELLIGENCE SUMMARY
(Erase heading not required.)

1/6 YORKSHIRE REGT.   Sheet No 2.

Place	Date	Hour	Summary of Events and Information	Remarks and references to Appendices
TRENCHES	1916 Sept 7	—	In trenches 9A in HULLUCH ALLEY. A quiet day. A very few T.M. came in, we see a few HULLUCH. Twenty rather [illeg.] not much to be seen, and a poor observation. All ground outside trenches made work going on well. [illeg.] almost work in the open in part [illeg.] line. The 110 Bde at 100 [illeg.]. The AntiAircraft Sappers from HULLUCH ALLEY to GORDON ALLEY under the new system of holding trenches. CL Col MATHIAS went on leave, command taken over by MAJOR V. FOWLER.	
do.	8	—	Still quiet & rather wet. Work proceeding satisfactorily, but a temporary dugout constructed by the R.E. in STANSFIELD WAY collapsed (twice). Two men of M Bay dug out in time.	
do.	9	—	A quiet day till about 1pm. The enemy then dropped about 15 - 4.2 shells (H) round EXETER CASTLE (Batt. HQ.) doing some damage & killing the ammunition cook, setting fire to VERY lights & ammunition. Quite exciting while it lasted. (c) wounded. No 120/10 Pte C.F. BARR.	
do.	10	—	A quiet morning. The Battn was relieved by "LINCOLN" complete 1pm. A/C.Coy who went to Reserve moved etc B+D Coys to CORNY C.[?] & QB.5. A/C Coy into billets at MAZINGARBE. EXETER CASTLE again at about 3 pm. The enemy appears block[?]	

WAR DIARY
or
INTELLIGENCE SUMMARY
(Erase heading not required.)

16 YORKSHIRE REGT.   Sheet No. 3

Army Form C. 2118

Place	Date 1916	Hour	Summary of Events and Information	Remarks and references to Appendices
TRENCHES	Dec. 11	-	In RESERVE trenches, a quiet day. (Ops at MAZINGARBE clammy etc. working parties as usual).	
do.	12	-	A rest too! day with some snow. Trenches rather bad. Work as usual.	
do.	13	-	Still damp & wet. A+C Coys relieved B+D Coys in O.B.S. a.m. Coys arrived, working parties as usual.	
do.	14	-	A quiet day, raining hard. Work as usual.	
do.	15	-	The Battn relieved the 1st LINCOLNS in front line trenches. 74 to HULLUCH ALLEY. Relief completed by 12.15 p.m. a quiet day and night.	
do.	16	-	Trenches 74 to HULLUCH ALLEY. A quiet day & night. Weather wet & fine. Working parties out (salvage) in 70 to 80 foot practically (as ld) trenches, a new day out of salvage parties.	
do.	17	-	A very quiet day & night except for enemy T.M. came over a few more shells. The enemy appear to be registering on various points. Work as usual.	

Army Form C. 2118

WAR DIARY
or
INTELLIGENCE SUMMARY

10 Yorkshire Sheet No 4.

(Erase heading not required.)

Place	Date	Hour	Summary of Events and Information	Remarks and references to Appendices
Trenches	Dec 18	—	In trenches 94th HULCH ALLEY. The enemy Rainforce his usual amount of T.M.S which we replied to by our machines & STOKES. Work as usual and trenches getting dryer.	
do.	19	—	do. The front line trenches were inspected by the G.O.C. 21 Division MAJOR GEN. D. CAMPBELL who was at the right of the Battn line at 8 AM. Weather turns cold & dry by midnight.	
do.	20	—	do. A very quiet day, fine, and work going on well.	
do.	21	—	do. Again a very quiet day, very cold and some incl T.M as usual.	
do.	22	—	do. Fairly quiet day, but rather more enemy shell fire than usual. He appears to be doing more registering. The Battn were relieved by the 1st LINCOLN REGT. relief completed at 12.45 pm. The Battn then relieved the 12. N.F. in support line. 17492 Pte H. Mc.LELLAN. (c) w. S.S. 5.12.16. 12141 „ H. NICHOLSON. (A) w. 19.12.16. 19642 „ W. BROWN. (A) w. do DEVON.	
do.	23	—	In Support trenches. The Battn H.Q. and district of Support Battn were shell(n) also DEVON LANE. Not much damage done. Whenever quiet, working parties Supplying 3635 - Pte. H. SYKES. (3) w.	

x1875 Wt. W 593/826 1,000,000 4/15 J.B.C. & A. A.D.S.S./Forms/C. 2118.

WAR DIARY or INTELLIGENCE SUMMARY

Army Form C. 2118

10 YORKSHIRE Regt. Sheet No 5

Place	Date	Hour	Summary of Events and Information	Remarks and references to Appendices
Trenches	1915 DEC 24	—	In Support trenches. A few more shells sent at H.Q. no damage, otherwise quiet during the night. Some 5" or 6" T.M. came from the SOUTH, not far away, it was obvious that we were raiding the enemy trenches.	
do.	25.	—	do. The day passed quietly, except for a few 7.7.cm. T.T.M being sent over, did night. Round fear fire T.M. came from the SOUTH. however was done, had a quiet night also.	
do.	26.	—	do. A quiet day, working parties as usual.	
do.	27.	—	do. The long looked for relief took place after the Brigade has been in the trenches once. Col. W.M. Prothers all the while we have been. The Brigade went relieved by the 4th Bgd. We to YORKS Regt. being relieved by the 2nd NOTTS & DERBY and it being completed by 7.0 pm a very slow relief, on relief the Batt marched to Billets at HOUCHIN. arriving there about 8.30 pm.	
HOUCHIN	28	—	In billets at HOUCHIN. The Batt moved up ready to move off at 10 am from the village, and marched to MARLES LES MINES. arriving there at 12.15 pm. and went into billets.	

Army Form C. 2118

WAR DIARY
or
INTELLIGENCE SUMMARY

(Erase heading not required.)

10 YORKSHIRE Regt.   Sheet No 6

Place	Date	Hour	Summary of Events and Information	Remarks and references to Appendices
MARLES	1915 Dec. 29.	—	In Billets men bathing and cleaning, inspection of Kits & saluting parade.	
do.	30	—	do. 2 hours work and saluting parade for junior Officers.	
do.	31.	—	do. Church Parade	

N. O.
Commanding. 10 Yorkshire Regt.

10th Yorkshire Regt. Army Form C. 2118

17.B.
5 sheets

Vol 17

WAR DIARY
or
INTELLIGENCE SUMMARY
(Erase heading not required.)

Place	Date	Hour	Summary of Events and Information	Remarks and references to Appendices
MARLES-LES-MINES (WITTLEBROUNE 6A)	JAN'Y 1st		Commencement of Bn. Training. Draft of 94 men arrived & were posted to Coys ("A" Coy 21, "B" Coy 26, "C" Coy 24, "D" Coy 23.)	
"	2nd		Bn. Training. Draft of 6 men arrived & were posted to Coys ("A" Coy 2, "B" Coy 2, "C" Coy 2, "D" Coy 2.).	
"	3rd		Nil.	
"	4th		Nil.	
"	5th		Bn. Route March. Lt: P.G.M. Sylvain proceeded on leave. The following were mentioned in Sir D. Haigs Despatch for the fighting on the SOMME:- Maj. F. Forster. No. 8671 R.S.M. HENDERSON.J. No. 1980. C.S.M. STANGROOM.S. No. 17526 SERGT. PEARSON.A. No. 130034 PTE. (A/CPL) WHISTER.G. (All 2 Bn.10.17.2.) Inspection of Bn. by C.O.	
"	6th		Church Parade.	
"	7th		Brigade Route March.	
"	8th		Bn. Training continued. The undermentioned Officers reported their arrival & were taken on the strength & posted to Companies as stated against their names:- Lt. N.E.S. GARDNER. M.C. ("C" Coy) 2nd Lt. J.C. STOREY. ("A" Coy) 2nd Lt. W.H. COKES. ("B" Coy) 2nd Lt. M.T.J. FAIRMAN. ("D" Coy)	
"	9th			

WAR DIARY or INTELLIGENCE SUMMARY

Army Form C. 2118

(Erase heading not required.)

Place	Date	Hour	Summary of Events and Information	Remarks and references to Appendices
MARLES-LES-MINES	JAN'Y 9th		Lt. H.F.S. GARDNER. M.C. assumed command of "C" Coy vice 2nd Lt. N.M. SLATER	
"	10th		Bn. in "Extended Order Drill in Woods." Lt. Col. G. Paley 2/10 N.W. arrived at AKKOUAGNE. Subject "The 910th Division."	
"	11th		Bn. Training & Bathing. Capt. W.H.G. GOATER reclined Lt. Col. C. Paley 2/10 N.W. 2nd in command. Capt. G.A. TURNER returned from 1st Army School & assumed command of "B" Coy. Lt. H.K. MARAND struck off strength, he proceeded to England, sick on 30/12/16.	
"	12th		Bn. Training & Bathing. Lt. J.P. PARKER assumed command of "D" Coy vice Capt. F.E.G. BAILEY to Course.	
"	13th		Inspection of Bn. by C.O. followed by Bn. Training. 2nd Lt. G.S. SARSON struck off strength from 3-1-17.	
"	14th		Church Parade. Capt. J.N. BARRACLOUGH struck off strength from 6-1-17.	
"	15th		Bn. Training. 2nd Lt. M. KEMP-WELSH proceeded on leave. Football Inter-Company match & stayed off. Rouen Bombers 2. "C" Coy O.	
"	16th		Bn. Route March. Lt. R.N. SYLVESTER returned from leave.	
"	17th		Inspection of Bn. by C.O.	

WAR DIARY
or
INTELLIGENCE SUMMARY

Army Form C. 2118

(Erase heading not required.)

Instructions regarding War Diaries and Intelligence Summaries are contained in F.S. Regs., Part II. and the Staff Manual respectively. Title Pages will be prepared in manuscript.

Place	Date	Hour	Summary of Events and Information	Remarks and references to Appendices
MARLES LES MINES	JANY 17th		Following extract from London Gazette 1/1/17 published:- No. 3/8755 C.S.M. J. McDONALD } Awarded " 1149 L. SERGE. J. DOWNING } D.C.M.	
"	18th		No. 26158. CPL. W. TANFIELD. died of wounds 7/1/17. Inspection by G.O.C. 62nd Inf. Brigade.	
"	19th		Bn. Training continued. 2nd Lt. J.L. Smith proceeds on tour.	
"	20th		Do. Bn. Cross Country run won was won off & rounded as follows:- 1st No. 6841 Pte. W. PRIOR. SNIPERS. (20 mins. 15 secs.) 2nd No. 19519 " W. CARTER. 'B' COY (20 mins. 17 secs.)	
"	21st		Church Parade. No. 2 Platoon "C" Coy. won place into Bn. Competition for best turned out Platoon. 'A' Coy Football team beat 'A' Coy 1st LINCOLNSHIRE REG.t in Semi Final by 3 goals to 1.	
"	22nd		Bn. training continued.	
"	23rd		Bn. Route March. Lecture by Lt. Col. BEAMAN. R.A.M.C. at ALLOUAGNE upon "His Experience as Prisoner of War in Germany." The undermentioned Officers reported arrival & were taken on strength:- 2nd Lt. G. BARTON ('B' COY) 2nd Lt. G. HARRIS ('C' COY)	

WAR DIARY
or
INTELLIGENCE SUMMARY

(Erase heading not required.)

Army Form C. 2118

Place	Date	Hour	Summary of Events and Information	Remarks and references to Appendices
MARLES-LES-MINES	JANY 24th		Bn. Training. "A" Coy Football team beat "B" Coy 13th N.F. by 2 goals to 1. Thus winning the Bde. Competition.	
"	25th		2nd LT. J.R. DOBINSON reported his arrival & was taken on the strength & posted to "A" Coy. Bn. Training.	
"	26th		Bn. Training. LT. T.J.S. PRATT and 2nd LT. G.N. MATHER proceed on leave. 2nd LT. W.M. SKATER assumes command of "A" Coy vice LT. T.J.S. PRATT.	
"	27th		Bn. Training. Bn. entrained at CHOQUES at 11.30 am for POPERINGHE.	
PESCHHOEK	28th		Detrained at POPERINGHE and marched to X CAMP PESCHHOEK. Church Parade.	
"	29th		Bn. Training.	
"	30th		Do. + Working Parties. Revue of Bde. H.Q. Guard Competition was made known as follows:- 12th N.F. ⎫ 13th N.F. ⎬ Equal First. 15th YORK.R ⎭ Remarks of G.O.C. 62nd INF. BDE. upon above were as follows:- "Each Guard was inspected by F.O.C. 62nd INF. BDE. The Brigade	

Wt. W593/826 1,000,000 4/15 J.B.C. & A. A.D.S.S./Forms/C. 2118.

WAR DIARY
or
INTELLIGENCE SUMMARY
(Erase heading not required.)

Army Form C. 2118

Place	Date	Hour	Summary of Events and Information	Remarks and references to Appendices
PETERHEAD	JANY 30/16		Major & the Staff Captain, & turned out at different times of the night, it was found impossible to say that any one of the above guards was any later than the others. The P.S.C. 62nd I.B. B.DE. considered that the Guards were a credit to their Bns. & congratulated their C.O.'s on their turn out, smartness & knowledge of their duties.	
"	31st		No parade. Working parties.	

W. H. G. Gada Capt.
O/C 1/5. Yorkshire Regt.

BATTALION ORDERS BY LT COL ...

10th Bn. YORKSHIRE REGIMENT.

1. Blankets rolled in bundles of to 9, and Campnow Stores etc. will be dumped at Quarter Master Stores by 10 a.m.

Two lorries will arrive about this hour and O.C. "D" Coy will detail a fatigue party of 1 N.C.O and 20 men to report in full marching order at 10 a.m. to load and unload blankets etc.

(Sgd) H.Bass Lt & Adjt
10. YORK. R.

18 B.
4 sheets

Army Form C. 2118.

10 Yorkshire Reg
21st November

Vol 18

WAR DIARY
or
INTELLIGENCE SUMMARY.
(Erase heading not required.)

Instructions regarding War Diaries and Intelligence Summaries are contained in F. S. Regs., Part II. and the Staff Manual respectively. Title pages will be prepared in manuscript.

Place	Date	Hour	Summary of Events and Information	Remarks and references to Appendices
FIELD	February 1917		Route March by Companies. Bn. returns 2 hours notice to move	
			Training and Company arrangements. 2/Lt S.L. SMITH returned from leave	
			Ditto	
			Church Parade. 2nd Lt O. GRENNWOOD joined Bn from	
			Base. Received order that Bn will be ready to move that bar	
			one Company and transport. Three miles away as a Reserve	
			Brigade, the Bn was ready to move at 11.25 am sharp and having	
			been served at 11.30 am. The Brigadier here confirmed the	
			C.O.'s orders on the movements and reports the position of	
			each company opposing 211th regmt to join our transport	
			N.K.	
			2nd Lt C.J. MATHER returned from leave	
			Bn in Billeting of reservation Trenches	
			Ditto	
			Various Parades.	

2353 Wt. W 2541/1454 700,000 5/15 D. D. & L. A.D.S.S./Forms/C. 2118.

Army Form C. 2118.

WAR DIARY
or
INTELLIGENCE SUMMARY.

(Erase heading not required.)

Instructions regarding War Diaries and Intelligence Summaries are contained in F. S. Regs., Part II. and the Staff Manual respectively. Title pages will be prepared in manuscript.

Place	Date	Hour	Summary of Events and Information	Remarks and references to Appendices
FIELD	February 1917			
	12th		Battalion training	
	13th		do	
	14th		do	
	15th		Bn. moved to 9 av 17. J.S. PRATT assumed Command from 2nd Lt.	
			Bn. marched to POPERINGHE & entrained for BETHUNE at 6 a.m.	Num Order No 22 attached
			Arrived BETHUNE at 12.15 p.m. & marched to BRIASTRE or ORPHANAGE	
	16th		Bn. moved to MAZINGARBE at 5.30 a.m. where Bn. relieved 1/4th	Nom Order No 23 attached
			NORFOLKS-LES-MINES, and went into trenches relieving the 9th	
			Bn. NORFOLK REGT. Relief complete by 12 noon. 1 O.R. & 2 O.R.	
			(wounded) admitted to hospital	
	17th		Bn. moved from MAZINGARBE at 5.30 am that relieved 1/4th	
			on trenches N.Q 1.N.5. (CARNES SECTOR) relief by 9h 2 RWK &	
			LEICESTER REGT. (acting) Bn. from a.s.s.B left 4th Bn. Relieved C.	
			Coys. SA 36. C N W). Relief complete at 12 noon	
			2nd LT. J. FAIRMAN wounded.	
	18th		The ordinary rounding occurred.	

WAR DIARY
or
INTELLIGENCE SUMMARY.

(Erase heading not required.)

Army Form C. 2118.

Place	Date	Hour	Summary of Events and Information	Remarks and references to Appendices
FIELD	February 19th 1917		* 770/41206 PTE. J. SANDERS "D" Coy Wounded.	
			" 41221 " W. RALPH "D" Coy "	
			" 41021 " F. KAY "B" Coy S.I.W.	
	20th		The following casualties occurred:-	
			No 36405 PTE. T. RIDSDALE "A" Coy Killed	
			" 36365 " T.W. MAXWELL "A" Coy Wounded	
			" 6669 SERGT. T. BUSH "A" Coy "	
			" 6653 PTE. WALSKIP "A" Coy "	
			" 57622 " J.J. THOMPSON "A" Coy "	
			* " 41206 PTE. J. SANDERS "D" Coy died of wounds received in action at No 22 C.C.S. Front line company right coy relieved by our left coy. Frequent enemy aeroplane activity Jas O Howard.	
			2nd Lt. L.P. CARRIER rejoined his arrival & was posted to "A" Coy CAPT. C.O. FORSTER & important reports to B Company. Recpt of 10 O.R. arrived & taken on strength of Bn.	

Army Form C. 2118.

WAR DIARY
or
INTELLIGENCE SUMMARY.

(Erase heading not required.)

Instructions regarding War Diaries and Intelligence Summaries are contained in F. S. Regs., Part II. and the Staff Manual respectively. Title pages will be prepared in manuscript.

Place	Date	Hour	Summary of Events and Information	Remarks and references to Appendices
FIELD	FEBRUARY 1917			
	21st		2/5 26550 PTE S. BICKERDIKE "A" Coy wounded	
	22nd		27/53 PTE A. CHILTON "A" Coy wounded taken by M.M. party in Empire	on patrol
	23rd		Nil	
	24th		MAJOR V. FOWLER Ganer off stringth (Sen. Off. (sick)) 2nd Lt. Q. GREENWOOD joined and posted to "B" Coy from Gazenbrook camp	
	25th		Quiet. Services. Bathing	
	26th		C.O.'s inspection of Companies.	
	27th		Bn. Training by Musketry (B) Physical Training (C) Bar. Exer. Drill. The following mountain opening upon date no others received. Various Games.	
			778/5136 PTE H. BRUNSKILL "A" Coy Wounded 25/2/17 W. WELLS "L" "C" Coy Wounded 24/2/17 3310-5	
	28th		Bn. moved to NOEUX-LES-MINES Billets	Minor dates noted attached
			FIELD 28/2/17	

A.W.G. Yeates Capt
10th Bn Yorkshire Regt

2353 Wt. W3544/1454 700,000 5/15 D. D. & L. A.D.S.S./Forms/C. 2118.

MOVE ORDERS 26.   SECRET
                  Copy No. 2
10h Bn. YORKSHIRE REGIMENT.   28.2.17.

1. 10 York. R. will move to billets at ROBECQ tomorrow March 1st, and will parade as detailed in Battn. Order No 3 of today's date.

2. Billeting party consisting of C.Q.M.Sgts, one representative from each Bombers, Signals, Transport, Bde H.Q. Platoon, and H.Q. together with the Interpreter and with 2/Lieut H.W.Bird in charge will parade at Orderly Room at 8.30 a.m.
   2/Lieut Bird, Sgt Shaw and the Interpreter will proceed by cycle, remainder marching there under senior N.C.O.
   Signal Officer will arrange to have three cycles at Orderly Room by 8.15 a.m.

3. Blankets rolled in bundles of tens and labelled, Officers Kits, Mens packs, Company stores etc. will be stacked on the square in front of Church by 10 a.m. The Regimental Guard found by "D" Coy will be in charge of same.
   Blankets and packs must, as far as possible be stacked and loaded by Coys in order to facilitate the re-distribution of same
   O.C. "C" Coy will detail a loading party of 1 N.C.O and 20 men to be on the Square at a time to be notified later. The Quarter Master will supervise loading of above.

4. Mess cart will collect Mess Baskets at 11.30 a.m.

                                    (Sgd) H.Bass Lt & Adjt
                                           10. YORK. R.

   DISTRIBUTION.
   No 1 File.
    2 War Diary.
    3 O.C. "A" Coy
    4 O.C. "B" "
    5 O.C. "C" "
    6 O.C. "D" "
    7 B.O.
    8 S.O.
    9 L.G.O.
   10 I.O.
   11 T.O.
   12 Q.M.
   13 M.O.
   14 Bde H.Q. Platoon.

Billets not available at ROBECQ. Bn. billets at L'ECLEME

WAR DIARY or **INTELLIGENCE SUMMARY.**

Army Form C. 2118.

10th Bn. Yorkshire Regt

MARCH 1917

Place	Date	Hour	Summary of Events and Information	Remarks and references to Appendices
FIELD	1st		Bn. marched from NOEUX-LES-MINES (map sh. 36 B N.E.) to and billeted at L'EULÈNE (map sh. 36 A S.E.)	2nd Lt. M. O. Page absent
	2nd		Bn. marched to & billeted at BUSNES (map sh. 36 A S.E.)	2nd Lt. O'Neal return
	3rd		NIL	2nd Lt. O Neil
	4th		Church parades	
	5th		Bn. Route March	
	6th		2nd Lt. W.H. COLES transferred from "B" Coy to "D" Coy	
	7th		Inspection of Bn. by Commanding Officer.	
	8th		Bn. Route March.	
	9th		2nd Lt. W.M. SLATER assumes command of "C" Coy vice 2nd Lt. K.L. HYANS. 2nd Lt. M.O. Nr 27 attached	
			Bn. marched to & billeted at AEOUNCHEL (map sh. HAZEBROUCK 5A)	
	10th		Bn. marched to & billeted at MARÊST (map sh. LENS II)	2nd Lt. M.O. No 20 attached
			2nd Lt. W.D. CHAMBERLAIN reports his return to Bn in Strength &	
			posted to "B" Coy.	
			26683 Pte H. SKIPP "A" Coy died of wounds received in action	
			8-3-17.	

19.13.
15 sheets

Army Form C. 2118.

WAR DIARY
or
INTELLIGENCE SUMMARY.
(Erase heading not required.)

Instructions regarding War Diaries and Intelligence Summaries are contained in F. S. Regs., Part II. and the Staff Manual respectively. Title pages will be prepared in manuscript.

Place	Date	Hour	Summary of Events and Information	Remarks and references to Appendices
FIELD	11th		Bn. marched to & billeted at FRAMECOURT and PETIT HOUVIN (map 51 LENS)	See M2 D, M2 SM attached. Ration Strength attached.
"	12th		Bn. marched to & billeted at BEAUREPAIRE (Map 5K LENS 11)	
"	13th		Bn. cleaning up	
"	14th		Bn. training	
"	15th		Ditto	
			LT. N.F.S. GARDNER M.C. struck off strength to Eng. Improvement Cen. as Instructor	
			2nd LT. G.H. MATHER ditto to Eng. sick 5/3/17	
			2nd LT. S.R. DOBINSON appointed Bn. Bombing Officer vice 2nd LT. T.R. EVANS	
			to Eng. 14/3/17 for permanent commission in Indian Army	
"	16th		Bn. practising "New Formation for Attack"	
"	17th		Ditto	
"	18th		Church Parade.	
"	19th		Bn. training	
"	20th		Bn. Route March	
"	21st		Do	
"	22nd		Bn. practising "new Formation for Attack"	

Army Form C. 2118.

WAR DIARY
or
INTELLIGENCE SUMMARY.
(Erase heading not required.)

Instructions regarding War Diaries and Intelligence Summaries are contained in F. S. Regs., Part II. and the Staff Manual respectively. Title pages will be prepared in manuscript.

Place	Date	Hour	Summary of Events and Information	Remarks and references to Appendices
FIELD	23rd		Bn. training	
"	24th		No parades. Summer time came into force on night of 24/25th	See N.O. ans attached
"	25th		Bn. marched to + billeted at BERLES-AU-BOIS (Map Sh. LENS 11)	
"	26th		NIL	
"	27th		Bn. marched to + bivouaced at HENDICOURT (Map Sh. LENS 11)	
"	28th		Bn. moved up to BOISLEUX-AU-MONT (Map Sh. LENS 11) + relieved the 2/5th LONDON REGT in support.	See O.O. No 35 attached
"	29th		Bn. supplied working parties.	
"	30th		Ditto. "A" + "B" Co'ys moved to BOYELLES — BOISLEUX-ST MARC approaches (map sh. 51B-S.W.) + 2nd Lt S. LUNEY proceeded on leave.	See O.O. No 35 attached
"	31st		NIL	

O. N. S. Goater Capt.
10th Bn Yorkshire Regt.

MOVT ORDERS 26 A   SECRET
Copy No..... 2
13th Bn. YORKSHIRE REGIMENT.   .17

1. 13 York. R. will move to BUSNES today and take over billets vacated by 11th Essex Regt.

2. Companies and Detachments will move off independently leaving present billets at 1.45 a.m. Dress Full Marching Order.

3. Billeting representatives will meet Companies and Detachments at the Cross Roads 1/8 mile due East of BUSNES Church.

4. Officers Kits will be at Quarter Master Stores by 11 a.m. Mess Buckets will be collected at 1.15 p.m.
Transport will move off at 1.30 p.m.

5. Whenever any move takes place O.C. Coys and Detachments will report present or otherwise as soon as possible after arrival in billets.

DISTRIBUTION.

No 1 Copy.   File.
   2   "   War Diary
   3   "   O.C. "A" Coy
   4   "   O.C. "B" "
   5   "   O.C. "C" "
   6   "   O.C. "D" "
   7   "   R.O.
   8   "   C.O.
   9   "   L.G.O.
  10   "   I.O.
  11   "   T.O.
  12   "   S.O.
  13   "   M.O.
  14   "   Bde H.Q. Platoon.

(Sgd) H.Case Lt & Adjt
13. YORK. R.

POST.   All letter for post to reach Orderly Room by 11 a.m.

```
              MOVE     ORDERS    27               SECRET
                                                  Copy No. 2
         10th Bn. YORKSHIRE REGIMENT              8.3.17
```

1. 62nd Inf. Bde. will march into the ST. HILAIRE Area tomorrow 9th inst.

2. Battalion will be formed up along the ST. VENANT - BUSNES Road with head of the column at the Church ready to move off at 11.40 a.m.
   Order of march - Signals, "A", "B", Drums, "C", "D", Details, and Transport.
   Route - LILLERS - ECQUEDECQUES - FANQUENHEM - AMES - AMETTES - Billets (NEDONCHELLE).

3. All blankets rolled in bundles of 10 will be at the Quartermaster's Stores by 10 a.m. O.C. "A" Coy will detail 1 N.C.O. and 20 men to load and unload these.
   All Coy stores will be at the same place at the same time.

4. The Mess Cart will collect mess baskets at 11 a.m.
   Maltese Cart will be at the Regimental Aid Post at 10 a.m.
   ½ Limber for Orderly Room stores, and ½ Limber for Canteen at 10 a.m.

5. All billets will be left clean and all chalk marks erased. A certificate that this has been done will be handed to the Adjutant at the head of the column at 11.40 a.m.

6. A billeting party of one representative per Coy and Signals will parade outside Bn Orderly Room at 8.30 a.m.

7. Officers valises will be at the Quartermaster's Stores by 10 a.m.

DISTRIBUTION

```
No   1  Copy    File
     2   "      War Diary
     3   "      O.C. "A" Coy
     4   "       "   "B"  "
     5   "       "   "C"  "
     6   "       "   "D"  "
     7   "      B.O.
     8   "      S.O.
     9   "      L.G.O.
    10   "      M.O.
    11   "      T.O.
    12   "      Q.M.
```

                                    (Sgd) H. Bass Lieut & Adjt
                                              10th YORK. R.

There will be no outgoing mail tomorrow.

MOVE ORDERS 30   SECRET
                         COPY No 2.
10th Bn YORKSHIRE REGIMENT   10.3.17

1. Battalion will be formed up at Road Junction 1/8 mile N of the second L in NEDONCHELLE along the road passing the Church ready to move off at 10.35 a.m. towards AUMERNAL
   Order of march - Signals, "B", "C", Drums, "D", "A", Details Transport.
   Dress - Full Marching Order.

2. Battalion will billet for the night in MAREST.

3. Billeting Party consisting of 2 representatives per Coy and Detachment will parade outside Bn Orderly Room ready to move off at 8 a.m. and will report to 2/Lieut W.H.Bird at the Church in MAREST at 10 a.m.

4. All blankets properly rolled, Coy stores will be at The Quartermaster Stores by 9.30 a.m. All Officers kits will be there at 9.30 a.m.
   Mess baskets will be collected at 9.30 a.m.

5. O.C. "A" Coy will detail a rear party of 1 Officer and 20 men for the march today.

6. Usual certificates as to the state of billets will be rendered.

7. Dinners will be carried on the cookers.

8. Sick parade will be at 7.30 a.m. There will be No Orderly Room.

DISTRIBUTION.

No	
1.	File.
2	War Diary
3	O.C. "A" Coy
4	O.C. "B" "
5	O.C. "C" "
6	O.C. "D" "
7	B.O.
8	S.O.
9	L.G.O.
10	I.O.
11	T.O.
12	M.O.
13	Q.M.

(Sgd) H.Bass Lt & Adjt
10. YORK. R.

MOVE ORDERS 31.   SECRET
                                    Copy No. 2...
10th Bn. YORKSHIRE REGIMENT.
_____

1. Battalion will be formed up at Road Junction 7/8th Mile
W.S.W. of the M in MAREST with head of column at the Road
junc. ready to move off at 8.30 a.m. towards ST POL.
Order of march - Signals, "C", "D" Coys Drums, "A", "B" Coys
                    Details, Transport.
Dress - Full marching order.

2. Battalion will billet in FRAMECOURT and PETIT NOUVIN.

3. Billeting party consisting of 2 representatives per Coy
and Detachments, including Transport will parade at Quarter
Master Stores at 8 a.m. and will proceed by the first two
Motors and will report to 2/Lieut H.W.Bird at the Church at
FRAMECOURT.

4. All blankets properly rolled and labelled, together
with Coy Stores will be stacked at Quarter Master Stores by
7.30 a.m. Officers kits will be stacked at the same place
and time.

5. Excluding the motor at present attached to the Battalion.
One Motor Lorry will be at PERNES Square at 8 a.m. and will be
brought along to the Quarter Master Stores. These lorries
are only allowed to carry half loads and to travel at 6 M.P.H.

6. Mess cart will collect Mess Baskets commencing at 7.30 a.m.

7. Dinners will be carried on cookers.

8. O.C. "B" Coy will detail a rear party of 1 Officer and
20 men for the March.

9. The Orderly Officer will remain behind for three hours
after the battalion leaves and will remain with the MAIRE to
meet any claims.
    O.C. Signals will arrange for cycle to be left for him.

10. Sick parade 7 a.m. Rum issue 6.30 a.m.

                                (Sgd) H.Bass Lt & Adjt
                                        10. YORK. R.
DISTRIBUTION
No 1 Copy.   File.
   2   "   War Diary
   3   "   O.C. "A" Coy
   4   "   O.C. "B" "
   5   "   O.C. "C" "
   6   "   O.C. "D" "
   7   "   B.O.
   8   "   S.O.
   9   "   L.G.O.
  10   "   I.O.
  11   "   T.O.
  12   "   Q.M.
  13   "   M.O.

MOVE ORDERS No 31. SECRET
                    COPY No. 2
10th Bn YORKSHIRE REGIMENT   12.3.17

1. The 62nd Inf. Bde. Group will march to the LUCHEUX Area today 12th ins

2. The Battalion less "A" & "B" Coys will be formed up on the road
leading from FRAMCOURT to Main Rd with head of column at Road
Junction ready to move off at 9.30 a.m.
   "A" & "B" Coys will be formed up with head of "A" Coy at the
place mentioned ready to move off at 9.30 a.m.
   Order of March - Signals, "D", "A", Drums, "B", "C" Coy, Details
and Transport. Dress - Full Marching Order.

3. Route - SERICOURT - SIBIVILLE - Riv Bdge ½ mile N. of C in
SERICOURT - X ROADS ½ mile N. of A in HORVAL - REBREUVE -
REBREUVIETTE- X ROADS 1/2 mile N of 1stE in REBREUVIETTE - X roads
N. of LE in LE SOUICH- X roads immediately N of Church at East of
GROUCHES- L'ESPERANCE.
   Transport will accompany unit until arrival at Church in GROUCHES
when it will follow the road Junc. 1/8 mile N. of LE in LE MARAIS
SEC- BEAUPAIRE

4. Battn will billet in BEAUPAIRE.

5. Dinners will be eaten on the road. A halt from 11.50 a.m. to 1.0p.m
will be made for this purpose.

6. Stores Officers Kits and Blankets of the Battn less "A" and "B"Coy
will be at he Quarter Mashers Stores by 8.0 a.m. The Stores Etc of
"A" and "B" Coy will be stacked in a place to be selected by O.C.
"B" Coy. A guard of 1 N.C.O and 3 men (those unfit for march should
be selected) to be detailed by O.C "B" Coy will be in charge of same.

7. Mess Cart will collect Mess Baskets of "A" and "B" Coys at 8.0a.m
It will then collect those in FRAMCOURT.

8. The Orderly Officer will report to the Mairie at SAINS and remain
with him for three hours to receive any claims against the Battn
He will then call at the Mairie at FRAMCOURT as he proceeds to
join the Battn .

9. Rear Guard of 1 Officer and 30 men will be detailed by O.C "C"Coy
This party will assist the transport when required and will be under
the orders of the transport Officer.

10. Billeting Party consisting of not more than 2 representatives
per Coy and Detachment will proceed by lorries as for Yesterday.
They will report to the Quarter Master at 8.45 a.m.

```
No 1 Copy File         No 8 Copy S.O.
"  2  "  War Diary     "  9  "  L.O.C.
"  3  "  O.C "A" Coy   " 10  "  I.O.
"  4  "   "  "B"  "    " 11  "  T.O.
"  5  "   "  "C"  "    " 12  "  Q.M
"  6  "   "  "D"  "    " 13  "  M.O.
"  7  "  B.O.
```

                              (Sgd) H.Bass Lt & Adj
                                      10 York R.

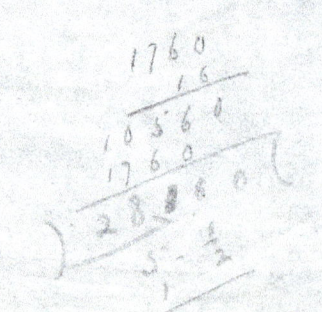

MOVE ORDERS No 32   Copy No. 2.
10th Bn. YORKSHIRE REGIMENT.   SECRET
25.3.17.

Map Ref. LENS 11.

1. The Battalion will move today 25th inst to BERLES AU BOIS area distance 12½ miles.

2. Battalion will be formed up ready to move off at 10 a.m. with head of column 800 yards East of BEAUREPAIRE on the DOULLENS - ARRAS Road.
Order of March - "B", "C", Drums, "D", "A" Coys, Details. Transport. Signals & Runners will lead.
Dress - Full marching order.

3. Route - MONDICOURT - PAS - HENU - SOUASTRE - Billets (BERLES AU BOIS)

4. All blankets properly rolled and labelled, Company stores & Officers valises will be at Quarter Master Stores by 9 a.m.
Two Lorries for carrying blankets will be at Q.M.Stores by 9 a.m.
A loading party consisting of 1 N.C.O and 20 men will be at Q.M.Stores at 9 a.m. Party will be detailed by O.C. "C" Coy.

5. Mess cart will collect Mess baskets at 9.15 a.m.

6. O.C. "A" Coy will detail a party of 1 Officers and 20 men to remain behind and see that billets are clean. The Officer will, prior to moving off obtain a certificate from the Town Major, HALLOY certifying billets to be clean.
Signal Officer will arrange for one cycle to be left with this party.

7. Rear Guard of 1 Officer and 30 men will be detailed by O.C. "A" Coy. This party will assist the transport when required & will be under the orders of the transport officer.

8. Billeting party consisting of 2/Lieut S.Loney, the Interpreter and two representatives per Company and Detachment will parade at Orderly Room at 9 a.m.

9. Dinners will be carried on cookers and served on arrival at New area.

10. Usual certificates on arrival in billets will be rendered.

DISTRIBUTION.

No 1 Copy.   File.
   2   "   War Diary
   3   "   O.C. "A" Coy
   4   "   O.C. "B" "
   5   "   O.C. "C" "
   6   "   O.C. "D" "
   7   "   B.O.
   8   "   S.O.
   9   "   L.G.O.
  10   "   T.O.
  11   "   Q.M.
  12   "   M.O.
  13   "   H.Q.Mess.

(Sgd) H.Bass Lt & Adjt
10. YORK. R.

OPERATION ORDERS No 33   Copy No. 2
                          SECRET
10th Bn. YORKSHIRE REGIMENT.   26.3.17.

1. Battalion will move into the line on Wednesday, 28th inst. and will relieve 2/5th London Regt in Support at BOISLEUX-AU-MONT.

2. (a) Company's will relieve the respective Company of the 2/8th(?) London R.

   (b) Order of March - "A", "B", "C", "D" Coys, H.Q. (includes Signals)

   (c) The First Company "A" Coy will pass Road junc. at W.21.b.0.8 at 12 noon and an interval of 500 yards between Coys will be observed until arrival at ADINFER, when an interval of 100 yards between platoons and 200 yards between Coys must be observed. Connecting files between platoons will be dropped at ADINFER.

   (d) Route - BIENVILLERS - AU - BOIS - MONCHY - AU - BOIS - ADINFER - SUGAR FACTORY (S.19.b.2.4.)

   (e) One guide per Company and one for Headquarters will await battalion at Sugar Factory

   (f) Dress - Full marching order.

3. Transport will move in rear of the Battalion and will proceed via the following route. BIENVILLERS AU BOIS - MONCHY AU BOIS - ADINFER - BOIRY ST MARTIN, where it remains
   Transport wagons will move in pairs with a distance of 100 yards between each pair

4. One blanket per man will be carried on transport, these will be rolled, labelled and dumped at Quarter Master Stores by 9 a.m on the morning of the 28th inst.
   The remaining blankets will be rolled, labelled and dumped at a place to be notified by the Quarter Master. A Guard of 1 N.C.O and 3 men to be detailed by O.C. "D" Coy will remain in charge of same, they must be rationed for 2 or 3 days if possible.
   Officers kits, and Company Stores will be dumped at Quarter Master Stores by 9 a.m on the 28th inst.
   Mess cart will collect mess baskets at 12 noon.

5. Dinners will be had before moving off and the remainder of days ration carried on the man.

6. At the first appearance of an aeroplane all troops will halt clear of the road and remain halted until the aeroplane has passed out of sight.

7. Completion of relief will be notified to Orderly Room by "Runner". H.Q. will be in a dugout in Sunken Road about S.16. Central.

DISTRIBUTION.
No	Copy	
1	"	File.
2	"	War Diary
3	"	O.C. "A" Coy
4	"	O.C. "B" "
5	"	O.C. "C" "
6	"	O.C. "D" "
7	"	B.O.
8	"	S.O.
9	"	L.G.O.
10	"	T.O.
11	"	Q.M.
12	"	M.O.
13	"	2/5th (?) London R.

(Sgd) H.Bass Lt & Adjt
10. YORK. R.

```
O.C. "A" Coy      R.O.
 "  "B"  "        S.O.
 "  "C"  "        L.G.O.
 "  "D"  "        M.O.
T.O.              Q.M.
War Diary
```

Reference attached O.O.

Battalion will march and bivouac for the night at ~~ADINFER~~. today 27th inst.

Reference order No 2 (c) "A" Coy will pass Road Junction at W 24.d.8.9. (Map 51c) at 11 a.m.

An advance party consisting of 2 representitives per Coy and Detachment under 2/Lieut S.Loney will leave Orderly Room at 8.30 a.m. and report to the Staff Captain at the Church in ADINFER at 10.30 a.m.

Mess Cart will collect mess baskets at 10 a.m.

Route - As given in O.O. 33

Oredrs for relief of the 2/5 Lnd Regt in BOISLEUX - AU - MONT will be issued on arrival at HENDECOURT.

Dinners will be served on arrival. Transport will accompany the Battn. and remain for the night at HENDECOURT.

In event of attack the line HAMELINCOURT - BOISLEUX- AU-MONT will be held.

(Sgd) H.Bass Lieut

27.3.17

OPERATION ORDERS No 34.   SECRET
10th Bn. YORKSHIRE REGIMENT   27.3.17.

Map Ref 51 b N.W.

1. Battalion will relieve 8/5th London Regt in BOISLEUX-AU-
MONT tomorrow 28th inst.

2. Battalion will move by platoons at 200 yards distance.
   Order of march "A", "B", "C", "D" Coys H.Q.
   First platoon of "A" Coy will leave lines at 8.45 a.m.

3. Route - Cross Country track to TWIN VALLEY, main Road to
   Road Junction S.14.c.4.7. along COJEUL RIVER VALLEY to
   BOISLEUX-AUMONT.

4. Transport will move by road via ADINFER to BOIRY ST MARTIN
   where it will bivouac.
      Guides for cookers and Company limbers will be at S.9.d.5.4
   at 11 a.m.
      One limber per Company and one for Headquarters will be
   loaded at Transport lines with officers trench kits, Company
   stores and everything required in trenches, by 8 a.m.
      Maltese cart with medical stores will also accompany
   transport for the trenches.
      All other stores which will not accompany battalion to
   trenches will also be at transport lines by 8 a.m.

5. One blanket per man will be brought up by transport to the
   trenches, these will be rolled, labelled & dumped at transport
   lines by 8 a.m. Remaining blankets will be kept at Quarter
   Master Stores at BOIRY ST MARTIN.

6. Dinners will be carried on the cookers and the remainder
   of days ration on the men.

7. Relief complete will be notified by runner to H.Q's
   in dugout on Sunken Road about S.16.Central.

8. Companies will relieve corresponding Coys of the 8/5th
   London Regt.

   DISTRIBUTION.

   No 1 Copy.   File.
      2   "   War Diary
      3   "   O.C. "A" Coy
      4   "   O.C. "B" "
      5   "   O.C. "C" "
      6   "   O.C. "D" "
      7   "   S.O.
      8   "   S.O.
      9   "   L.G.O.
     10   "   T.O.
     11   "   I.M.
     12   "   M.O.
     13   "   M.O.Mess
     D9

                        (Sgd) H.Bass Lt & Adjt
                              10. YORK. R.

OPERATION ORDERS No 35.   Copy No. 2
SECRET
10th Bn. YORKSHIRE REGIMENT.
30.7.17.

Map Ref. 51.b.S.E.

1. "A" & "B" Coys will move to BOYELLES and BOISLEUX ST MARC respectively tonight. Companies will move by platoons at 200 yards interval "A" Coy leading. First platoon will move off at 8 p.m.

2. Blankets of "A" & "B" Coys will not be taken. Packs will be taken
   their
3. "A" & "B" Coys will leave a carrying parties of 16 O.R. at old Battalion H.Q. in S.16.a.9.5.

4. Blankets of "A" & "B" Coys will be rolled in bundles of tens, stored and stacked at Regimental Aid Post at BOISLEUX AU MONT. The 16 men left behind will load these on returning ration wagons.

5. Each man moving forward will carry 50 rds extra S.A.A to be drawn from Bn. H.Q. S.16.a.9.3. this afternoon.

6. Battalion Reserve of Bombs at present with transport will be taken to new Battn. H.Q. tonight S.11.d.3.4 (Old 13th N.F. H.Q.)

7. Battalion H.Q. will move to the old 13th N.F. H.Q at S.11.d.3.4. at 8 p.m tonight.

8. Mess baskets can be sent back by ration wagons tomorrow night.

9. Rations for "A" & "B" Coys tonight will be brought up to dump at S.11.c.9.3, where the BOISLEUX AU MONT - BOISLEUX ST MARC Road crosses the Railway
   Companies will arrange to have ration parties there at a time to be notified later.

10. Relief complete will be notified by runner to New Bn. H.Q. when "A" & "B" Coys are in position.

11. The following officers will return to transport lines tomorrow night, they may accompany Coys tonight.
    Capt W.H.C.Coster.   Capt
    Capt G.A.Turner. O.C. "B" Coy
    2/Lieut L.I.Collins 2nd in Command "A" Coy
       "   W.Pepper   Reserve S.O.
       "   L.P.Carrier   "   B.O.

12. "A" & "B" Coys will take forward Dixies, Cookers will be taken to Transport lines tonight.

(Sgd) H.Bass Lt & Adjt
10. YORK. R.

DISTRIBUTION.
No 1 Copy.   "A" File.
   2   "   War Diary.
   3   "   O.C. "A" Coy
   4   "   O.C. "B" "
   5   "   O.C. "C" "
   6   "   O.C. "D" "
   7   "   B.O.
   8   "   S.O.
   9   "   L.G.O.
  10   "   T.O.
  11   "   Q.M.
  12   "   M.O.
  13   "   H.Q.Mess.

WAR DIARY or INTELLIGENCE SUMMARY

Army Form C. 2118.

10th Yorkshire Regt. Sheet No. 1.

Vol 2 Q

20 B
5 sheets

Place	Date	Hour	Summary of Events and Information	Remarks and references to Appendices
In the field	1917 April 1	-	The Battn. moved to Railway Embankment at T.20.d at dusk. Details left at BOIRY ST. MARTIN	
do.	2	-	Zero hour 5.15 a.m. The Battn. remained at entrenchment all night reached A.T.B. Obj° to reinforce 13 NORTH'LD FUSRS guard N. of CROISELLES. at night the Battn. relieved the 13 N.F.	
do.	3	-	In the early morning Battn. pushed patrols through CROISELLES and occupied Hillside forming up N. of Ausneville night reinforced by 2 companies. (Continued consolidating. Battn was relieved by the 6th LEICESTER. REGT. Battn. moved back to hut lies in HAMLINCOURT.	
do.	4	-		
do.	5	-	Battn. moved to billets in ADINFER. practically no cover at all for personnel and weather very bad. all the time. C & D Coys were left on RAILWAY EMBANKMENT. at S.22.d under orders of NO 6 Coy Rgt.	
ADINFER	6	-	Battn. resting	
do.	7	-	do	
do.	8	-	Battn moved to BOISLEUX-AU-MONT into bivouacs. Details left at DINFER.	
In the field	9	-	Battn. moved to BOIRY BECQUERELLE and was joined by C & D Coys by light railway in two parties. O.C. Wn. (sic) taken over Q.20.W. S.E. of HENIN-SUR-COJEUL in prep. for an OFFENSIVE

WAR DIARY
INTELLIGENCE SUMMARY

(6 YORKSHIRE. REGT.)

Sheet No 2.

Army Form C. 2118.

Place	Date	Hour	Summary of Events and Information	Remarks and references to Appendices
In the Field	1917 Oct 10	—	Batt. at HEMIN under orders of 64 Inf Bgd. about 11 am we came under Artillery fire by 2 Inf Bgd (our own) and the Batt. were ordered to attack in conjunction with the 1st LINCOLN REGT. on the following day, objective HINDENBURG LINE	
do.	11	—	At 6 am. The Batt. attacked the objective and failed to force an entrance to the enemy line owing to the thickness of wire which was uncut by our own artillery. Lieuts. PRATT. and KEMP-WELCH. Killed. Cpl. BAILEY. Cpl. SHORT. and 2/Lt. COLES. wounded. about 120 other ranks. killed and wounded. That night the Batt. was relieved by the 13 N.F. & moved into reserve at BOIRY. BECQUERELLE.	
BOIRY. BECQUERELLE	12	—	Batt. resting	
do.	13	—	Batt. moved forward to HEMIN — COBRELLES. and in reserve, at night H.Q. & B I D Coy moved back to BOIRY. BECQUERELLE	
do.	14	—	Batt. resting. were relieved by A.Y.C. & in evening of 14th.	
do.	15	—	Batt. moved to billets at BEAUMETZ.	
BEAUMETZ	16	—	Batt. in billets resting & re-fitting. The Details left ADINFER. and rejoined the Batt.	
do.	17	—	do. weather very wet and cold.	

WAR DIARY
or
INTELLIGENCE SUMMARY.

(Erase heading not required.)

Army Form C. 2118.

to YORKSHIRE REGT. Sheet No 3

Place	Date	Hour	Summary of Events and Information	Remarks and references to Appendices
BEAUMETZ	1916 Oct/18	—	Batt. in billets - resting - weather still very wet.	
do.	19	—	do	
do.	20	—	do. inspection of Coys by C.O. and training afternoon.	
do.	21	—	do. Training took under Coy. C.O.'s Specialist Officers. 2nd Lt. T. PEARSON, W.E.A. OXLEY & M.L. TOBLE reported for duty	
do.	22	—	do. with the Battn.	
do.	23	—	do. Church Parade	
do.	24	—	Battn moved at 5.30 A.M. and marched to MERCATEL the details left behind moved to BLAIRVILLE arriving 9 at 9 A.M. A & D were billetted in huts in QUARRY near village	
MERCATEL	25	—	Battn in support of 20 Division Details at BLAIRVILLE	
do.	26	—	Battn moved to BOIRY BECQUERELLE in reserve to own Division (21st) which moved into BOIRY BECQ. area after 20th Division.	
BOIRY BECQUEREL	27	—	Battn in reserve. Details moved from BLAIRVILLE to BOIRY BECQ 2 moves after dark	
do.	28	—	do. Coys in the attack	
do.	29	—	do. Battn relieved the 9th LEICESTER REGT in front line relief complete at 11.30pm front line area from U.13.c.8.3. to T.11.d.q.1. Battalion moved with Headquarters Coys. the majors 51.B.S.W.	
in the field	30	—	Battn in front line trenches all quiet	do —

T.G. Matheson
O.C. ??? Yorkshire Regt

WAR DIARY
or
INTELLIGENCE SUMMARY.
(Erase heading not required.)

Army Form C. 2118.

10th Yorks Regt
Vol 21

Place	Date	Hour	Summary of Events and Information	Remarks and references to Appendices
A.H. Bd.H	1915 Aug 1		Batn in Bivouac as before. Fairly quiet. Divine Service.	
do	2		do	
do	3		do	
do	4		Col. Chadwick reported for duty with Battn	
do	5		2/Lt L Martin	
do	6		Battn in Bivouac. Remain same place. Weather hot & dry	
do	7		do	
do	8		do	
do			enlarged dugouts begun near 76.34. m. (T.27.c.1.9) and so on. Relief complete at 12 midnight.	
do	9		Col. Thomson appointed brig. of B. Battery near Bois Fm. Col F.W. Harris took over duty. H.Q. B.H.	
do	10		do	
do	11		do	

Army Form C. 2118.

WAR DIARY
or
INTELLIGENCE SUMMARY

(Erase heading not required.)

Instructions regarding War Diaries and Intelligence Summaries are contained in F. S. Regs., Part II. and the Staff Manual respectively. Title pages will be prepared in manuscript.

Place	Date	Hour	Summary of Events and Information	Remarks and references to Appendices
HEADQRT	13			
do	14			
do	15			
do	16			
do	17			
do	18			
do	19			
do	20			
do	21			
do	22			
do	23			

Army Form C. 2118.

WAR DIARY
or
INTELLIGENCE SUMMARY.
(Erase heading not required.)

10th Yorkshire Regt

Instructions regarding War Diaries and Intelligence Summaries are contained in F.S. Regs., Part II. and the Staff Manual respectively. Title pages will be prepared in manuscript.

Place	Date	Hour	Summary of Events and Information	Remarks and references to Appendices
HENDECOURT	1917 Mar 24	—	Working on defences.	
do	25	—	Soft March in morning for a — service for all officers & men 147 Coy.	
do	26	—	Snow coming. 7 K Coy.	
do	27	—	Coy training in fire orders use of Lewis gun & Lewis bomb in the trenches	
do	28	—	Church parade. Practice attack by 11 officers.	
do	29	—	Coy training and stunt programmes. Rod for 1/4/17	
do	30	—	Bayonet fighting, Practice attack for officers. Working parties.	
do	31	—	Bnd obey roam 5 30 pm to 10 pm. Coy training Battn. Practice attack for officers Working Parties Bayonet fighting. Lectures by Coy.	
do	April 1	—	Battn. moved from HENDECOURT at 5 p.m. to relieve the 9 H.L.I. in Support. heades at U.13.A.9.0. Support trenches run from U.13.c.7.5 to U.13.a.7.3 Battn. H.Q. at U.13.a.7.1. relief complete at 11.30. p.m.	

V. Fowler
Major
Comdg. 10 Yorkshire Regt.

Army Form C. 2118.

WAR DIARY
or
INTELLIGENCE SUMMARY.
(Erase heading not required.)

10th Yorkshire Regt.

JUNE 1917   Vol 22

Place	Date	Hour	Summary of Events and Information	Remarks and references to Appendices
FIELD	1st	—	In support trenches. Quiet day. Improving trenches. Being used by Bn. front and wiggen? Communication trenches to front line.	
	2nd	—	Our trenches heavily shelled with 7.9 on shells causing following casualties.	
			No 18042 Pte. CUMMINGS H.A. "C" COY KILLED.	
			" 33145 Pte SPINKS R. "B" COY DIED OF WOUNDS	
			" 15840 " BROWN. J.R. "B" COY WOUNDED	
			" 33020 " McELROY " "B" COY "	
			" 33145 " BEASLEY. H. "B" COY "	
			" 33206 " EDMONSON H. "C" COY "	
			" 33191 " PIPER J.W. "C" COY "	
			" 33183 L.CPL. BAKER. E.E. "C" COY S.SHOCK	
			" 20325 PTE. ROBINSON G "C" COY "	
			Trenches were shelled during day again 7.7 cm & 15 cm shells cir 8.30 pm the following casualties occurred.	
			MAJOR V. FOWLER KILLED	
			No 14169 SERGT DOWNING J "C" COY KILLED	

Army Form C. 2118.

WAR DIARY
or
INTELLIGENCE SUMMARY.
(Erase heading not required.)

Place	Date	Hour	Summary of Events and Information	Remarks and references to Appendices
FIELD	2nd	1	Capt. W.H.G GOATER took command of the Battalion & 2nd Lt W.M. SEATH of C Coy took over Capt W.H.G GOATER	
"	3rd	1	Work on trenches proceeded well. Intermittent shelling all day. 2nd Lt O.S. SASSON rejoined his unit.	
"	4th	1	Taken on strength & posted G/ B Coy for duty. Trench held by A Coy on U.13.c (37.B SW)d were heavily shelled & the Coy withdrawn to an old trench behind the quarry on T.18.D.(17.5.m). The following casualties occured:-	
			N° 28576 PTE BOTTOM O.W. A'COY KILLED	
			8089 L.CPL. HARDING J.R. A'COY WOUNDED	
			13719 PTE FAIRCLOUGH J. A'COY "	
			18016 PTE GREY T. A'COY S. SHOCK	
			17313 " BULMER J.W. A'COY S. SHOCK (a-R.y)	
			6997 " DONERLY L. A'COY S. SHOCK	
"	5th	1	Early quiet day. Party working on trail of Lund Lane & C Coy digging LUMP LANE	

Place	Date	Hour	Summary of Events and Information	Remarks and references to Appendices
FIELD	6th	—	Shelling continued during the day. During Coy relief 2 men wounded of GUARDIAN TRENCH & QUARRY garrison. Shelling heavier during evening. Following casualties occurred. Capt W.H.G. COATER wounded (at duty) No 17326 C.Q.M. Sergt RICHENS J. "C" Coy wounded 41856 Pte HARRIS "C" "C" Coy wounded (at duty)	
FIELD	7th	—	Work on new workmans continued. Bn relieved by 7th Bn LEICESTER REGT on evening of 7th and took to Sec Crk 93 "O" Camp MOYENNEVILLE (less "B" & "D" Coys) "B" & "D" Coys remained 62.69² in SUNKEN RD in T.28.C. (51.B.S.W.) & supplied working parties for the front line.	
FIELD	8th	—	Bn cleaning up. Lt Col. T.G. MATHIAS (from leave) assumed command of Bn vice Capt W.H.G. COATER. M.C. who assumed Comd no 2 Coy "C" vice Maj V. FOWLER (killed in action) 7-6-17. Capt A.H. ADWICK resumed command of "C" Coy vice Lt W.M. SLATER	
FIELD	9th	—	"A" & "C" Coys inspected by the Commanding Officer.	

WAR DIARY
or
INTELLIGENCE SUMMARY.
(Erase heading not required.)

Army Form C. 2118.

Place	Date	Hour	Summary of Events and Information	Remarks and references to Appendices
FIELD	10th	—	Church Parade.	
	11th	—	"A" & "C" Companies bathing.	
	12th	—	"A" & "C" Companies returned. "B" & "D" Companies ditto. Sunken Road on T.31.c.	
	12th	—	Bn. cleaning up. No. 26620 Pte. Watson R.E. "A" Coy. wounded.	
	13th	—	"B" & "D" Coys inspected by the Commanding Officer.	
	14th	—	Bn. training. Relieving – 1 Officer, 6 other ranks detailed Preliminary attack. 2nd Lt. H. Hume reported has arrived taken on strength & posted to "A" Coy.	
	15th	—	Bn. training – Practice of attack formations. No. 33162 Pte. Fowler H. "B"(C)(?) wounded at/shot. C.H. Perkins proceeded on leave. Bn. moved up in relief "B" & "D" Coys to St. Leger Camp. "A" & "C" remained in reserve at camp. Position Bn. H.Q. on T.22.	See O.S. list
	17th	—	Bn. on working parties near front line.	
	18th	—	Ditto.	
	19th	—	Bn. moved back (by Railway) to Bellacourt & billeted there. No. 3370 Pte. Cross G.O. "C" Coy. wounded. No. 96620 Pte. Fairweather J.R. "B" Coy. wounded (at duty).	See O.S. list it attained

T2134. Wt. W708—776. 500000. 4/15. Sir J. C. & S.

Army Form C. 2118.

WAR DIARY
or
INTELLIGENCE SUMMARY.
(Erase heading not required.)

Instructions regarding War Diaries and Intelligence Summaries are contained in F. S. Regs., Part II. and the Staff Manual respectively. Title pages will be prepared in manuscript.

Place	Date	Hour	Summary of Events and Information	Remarks and references to Appendices
FIELD	19th		PTE WALSH C. W. WOUNDED (AT DUTY)	
	20th		Bn. cleaning up.	
	21st		Parade rehearsal. Company arrangements. Special attacking party training. Evening Officers & NCOs talking at St Luers Common. Command of "A" Coy with Capt T.R. Short (on leave).	
	22nd		"A" & "B" Coys Transport inspected by Commanding Officer	
	23rd		"C" & "D" Coys inspected by Commanding Officer	
	24th		Church Parades	
	25th		2nd LT. C. W. HOOD on leave.	
	26th		Bn. Training. Attack formation. Visibility Societies and NCOs & Officers. Dr. P.T. Geo Smith – Macon Coy – L.V. Smith to lead	
	27th		Bn. Route March. BEAUCOURT – BERTVILLES – LE FRESNOY – RIVIERE –	
	28th		Bn. cleaning up.	
	29th		Bn. moved to BULLECOURT by train & motor bus	
	30th		Bn. relieved the 11th Bn. SUFFOLK – REGT in front line N.E. FONTAINE-LES-CROISILLES	12. M. O. S. attached S.O.S. attn

W.W.G. Carroll Major
10th Bn Yorkshire Regiment

30/6/17

WAR DIARY or INTELLIGENCE SUMMARY

Army Form C. 2118.

10th Bn Yorkshire Regt

Vol 2 3

23.B.
7 shell

JULY 1917

Fine day in trenches. Much work done in trenches and wiring.

Serjeant H.J. MARSDEN & 6 O.R.s wounded.

9 OR FRONTIER. Tour of Trenches (20-6-17)

D. Coy relieved A Coy Pts & LPts 1 Bn YORKSHIRE REGT in BROWN TRENCH.

Enemy artillery active.

Much work done in improving the trenches.

B Coy relieved C Coy of the 1 LANCASHIRE REGT in KEMA TRENCH.

tonight – 15.7.17 – C Coy 0 N.C.O's (8 others) have relieved D Coy in CLAY TRENCH & we moved back to KING TRENCH.

Following message received from G.O.C from Brigadier General:
(sent ? June 1917) BDE: "Please convey my congratulations to all officers
on their anniversary of their gallant achievement in the capture of
WOOD (94) (C.G. Rowley) Brig General.

The following m.g. wind came: "The Lieutenant Officer at Officers and Other Ranks wish to thank the Extreme..."

WAR DIARY
or
INTELLIGENCE SUMMARY.

(Erase heading not required.)

Army Form C. 2118.

Place	Date	Hour	Summary of Events and Information	Remarks and references to Appendices
FIELD	5th		Refer to the reconstructions which are shewn approved by the Four (4) of J.J. Marks & 2nd Lieut Watts Yellow Flag. M2-235097 Pte JONES F. Hurt of wounds 10·05 2nd Lt Wm. ALLIS injured this evening from a fall obtained 1 pm on tour point G.D. Company. The days command has been taken over & hearing of latrine opening Diseases two holes on day common run own on June end trenches. |		
	7th		NS-20277 Pte PURVIS T. D. Coy Employed. No.4160 Pte JONES R.C. C. Coy (24) killed on wiring party. 2nd Lt I.H. PERKINS transferred to C.Coy moving to akers Co. 2nd Lt J.G. JOBY (Asst Camp). |		
	8th		2nd Lt A.W. BIRD appointed Adjutant in J. Bowen's place NO-25076 Pte. BATES F. D. Coy wounded. Battalion relieved by 10th Bn. NORTHUMBERLAND Fusiliers |	attached

Army Form C. 2118.

WAR DIARY
or
INTELLIGENCE SUMMARY.
(Erase heading not required.)

Instructions regarding War Diaries and Intelligence Summaries are contained in F. S. Regs., Part II. and the Staff Manual respectively. Title pages will be prepared in manuscript.

Place	Date	Hour	Summary of Events and Information	Remarks and references to Appendices
FIELD	8th		Bnd. word took over support trenches vacated [illegible] and moved into working parties	for [illegible] [illegible] corrected attached
"	9th		MILITARY MEDAL awarded to Nº 35042 Pte HOWES on 9-9-17 for action on 11 working in relieved and [illegible] that the party were [illegible] the trench. The incident when ??, with great coolness the grenade and [illegible] off, ran to the parapet & [illegible] it [illegible] [illegible] [illegible] up a shower of earth to the parapet & were it exploded. Pte [illegible] own coolness and [illegible] saved the lives of him comrades who were now working in the trench not two yards distance. [illegible] returned on support trenches & [illegible] [illegible] working parties	
"	10th		None working and wiring party	
"	11th		Ditto	
"	12th		Ditto	
"	13th		Ditto	
"	14th		Enemy artillery action on HIND TRENCH in the morning	

WAR DIARY
or
INTELLIGENCE SUMMARY.

Army Form C. 2118.

Place	Date	Hour	Summary of Events and Information	Remarks and references to Appendices
FIELD	14th		Following casualties occured:-	
			770. 16979 Sergt O'Brien. J. D. Coy Wounded (At Duty)	
			" 41892 Pte Julley. J. D. Coy Ditto	
			" 41893 Pte Kaltenbaur G. D. Coy Wounded	
	15th		Quiet day. Found working & wiring parties	
	16th		Battalion relieved by the 9th Bn K.O.Y.L.I. and marched out to the O.S.N.S	(see app.) attached
			"C" Camp Moyenneville (Map Sh 51 B S.W.)	
	17th		Battalion cleaning up and bathing	
	18th		All Roll Proprietors of Battalion held in two Churches	
	19th		2nd Lt C.H. Perkins returned to "B" Coy for duty	
			2nd Lt J.C. Story returned from Rest camp	
			2nd Lt D.C. Beenwood transferred to D Coy for duty	
	19th		Inspection of "C" & "D" Coys by Commanding Officer	
			Company training	
	20th		Inspection of A & B Coys by 2nd in Command and B Coy Commanding Officer. Company training	

WAR DIARY
or
INTELLIGENCE SUMMARY.

(Erase heading not required.)

Army Form C. 2118.

Place	Date	Hour	Summary of Events and Information	Remarks and references to Appendices
FIELD	20th		Bn. went into [trenches] north [of] road opp. to the line from [Givenchy]. 2nd Lt. G.A. BOWKER & 2nd Lt. J.T. HUMPHREYS reported their arrival from the [reserve]. 2nd Lt. [Lt] was sent home to [ordnance] respectively.	
"	21st		Officers moved through a Lecture [Service] of R.O.A. Shot O.V. Church Parade.	
"	22nd		Capt. H RMS returned from leave & assumed command [pending] 2nd Lt. H.W. BIRD assumed duties as [Bn. Adjutant].	
"	23rd		[C] [Morning] Bn. [went] out [and] moved [notice] to [move] up to the line from [6pm]. rendel 6 p.m. on 24th.	
"	24th		Bn. relieved 9/Bn. K.O.Y.L.I. in Right Sub Sector.	S.O. [attached] [attached]

WAR DIARY
or
INTELLIGENCE SUMMARY.

(Erase heading not required.)

Army Form C. 2118.

Place	Date	Hour	Summary of Events and Information	Remarks and references to Appendices
FIELD	25th		CAPT. O.B. PARSONS proceeded on leave.	
"	26th		Following reported officially as prisoners of war in Germany:- No. 16906 SERGT. DONEGHAN. J. "C" Coy at LOMBARD. 12454 PTE. KENNEDY. L. "C" Coy at BELFIX DULMEN. 2nd LT. J.C. STORY assumed command of "A" Coy vice LT. L.L. COLLINS (rest camp). Following promotions appeared in London Gazette of 22/9/17:- TEMP. LT. W.M. SLATER to be TEMP. CAPT. 0/26/5/17. TEMP 2ND LT. F.P. CHIPP to be LT. LIEUT. 0/27/3/17. TEMP 2ND LT. E. PEPPER to be TEMP. HEUT. 0/27/8/17.	
"	27th		SERGT. R.W. KITCHING. "B" Coy KILLED. PTE. ANNIS acting as CPL on LEWIS GUN (from Canal).	
"	28th		CAPT. J.A. SHORT acquired command of "A" Coy vice 2nd LT. J.C. STORY. No. 41799 PTE. MARRIE. H.A. "A" Coy WOUNDED	
"	29th		CAPT. R. STOWERS proceeded on leave.	
"	30th		Quiet day.	
"	31st		A most successful raid was carried out by a party from B Battalion	

WAR DIARY or INTELLIGENCE SUMMARY

Army Form C. 2118.

Place	Date	Hour	Summary of Events and Information	Remarks and references to Appendices
FIELD	30/31		At 2 am on night 30/31 the Scheme attached	
			a very important identification was obtained. The only casualties sustained were an N.C.O. missing & one man slightly wounded. The latter not belonging to the raiding party.	
			The party was joined by C/Coy & commanded by 2/Lt J.L Smith. *Report*	
			2nd Lt. H.E. READ, and gained ranging. was shewn by 2/Lt J.L. Smith	
			occurred in a sharp fight at close quarters with the enemy.	marked □
			The casualties were. C/Coy —	
			No. 13643 CPL. MURRAY J. C/Coy MISSING	
			" 25641 PTE. MIDDLETON G.S. D/Coy WOUNDED.	
			MAJOR. W.H.G. CARTER M.C. assumed command of the Bn. vice Lt. Col.	
			T.G. MATTHEWS. D.S.O. on temp. command of Bde. vice 2nd i/c.	
	31/7/17			

W.H.G. Carter Major Comdg
10th Bn. Yorkshire Regiment.

WAR DIARY
INTELLIGENCE SUMMARY

10th B. Yorkshire Regt.
AUGUST 1917
Vol 24

24.B.
7 sheets

Place	Date	Hour	Summary of Events and Information	Remarks and references to Appendices
FIELD	1st	-	Battalion relieved by 2nd Yorkshire and Foreign Bn ... camp at ROYON...	
"	2nd	-	Battalion cleaning up and Baths	
"	3rd	-	(C) Training (D) Cos... early Engineer... Final for Lewis Gunners Groups	
"	4th	-	(B) Training as above. 2/Lt J. BRYAN and 2/Lt ZAHRSOO reported arrived from... Joined to B & H Pt respectively	
			No. 4188 A/Cpl MAXWELL A.J. killed	
			12781 Pte LYNN M	
			53205 " LOFT T.W. } C (C? wounded	
			53202 " METCALF W	
			26621 " TURNER C.W.	
"	5th		Church Parade. No. 6601 Pte TURNER C.W. (C) died of wounds	
"	6th		Lt & QM R Cunning proceed on Leave	
			NE 94129 Pte HAYTON R.C. A/CQMS officially appointed CQMS of A Co	
			Capt & Adj J. Thompson assumed command of A Co, 2nd Lt Cook F.R. Croisette (not camp)	

Army Form C. 2118.

WAR DIARY
or
INTELLIGENCE SUMMARY.
(Erase heading not required.)

Place	Date	Hour	Summary of Events and Information	Remarks and references to Appendices
FIELD	6th	—	Coy training.	
	7th		Coy training. Maneuvres. Acting Past Adjutancy Divisional Ride been gained by Corps Commander.	
			BAR TO MILITARY MEDAL	
			No 12047 Sergt. Lane E.A. C Coy	
			MILITARY MEDAL	
			No 18979 Sergt. J. O'Brien D Coy	
			" 13918 " E.W. Jones E Coy	
			" 17519 " T. Hirst C Coy	
			" 33205 Cpl. A. Dykes C Coy	
			" 33198 L/Cpl. E. Laing C Coy	
			Personal Foot inspection. Letter received 9th Battn. K.O.Y.L.I. in	Lt. Farrar (?) N.S. 67 attached
			Brigade Reserve	
	8th		Rest day.	
	9th		Bn relieved by 9th Battn Leicester Regt & marched back to B'Hopp.	La Butte
			MOYENNEVILLE. (Two working parties)	N.S. 5 attached

Place	Date	Hour	Summary of Events and Information	Remarks and references to Appendices
FIELD	9th		21st DIV. SPECIAL ORDER Initialled:- The General Officer Commanding the [Division?] has much pleasure in publishing the following note from the Army Commander but cannot let the opportunity pass without [adding?] his own [thanks?] to all ranks & the Corps Commander and the pleasure of saying how he [values?] the confidence of the Corps Commander. "On relief of the Corps H.Q. I write to you to convey to you all ranks of all arms of the 21st Division Van Hugh [Gough's?] appreciation of the most excellent service rendered by the Division during its long stay with the Corps. The splendid [offensive?] spirit which the [Division] always showed in the trenches has been more than justified by the performance of all ranks both in the ARRAS battle and in the subsequent pursuit up of the lost line. The [solidity?] of the line now being handled over to the VII Corps is proof of the high quality of the [troops] now now handed of who bear so distinguished a part in winning it."	

Army Form C. 2118.

WAR DIARY
or
INTELLIGENCE SUMMARY.
(Erase heading not required.)

Instructions regarding War Diaries and Intelligence Summaries are contained in F. S. Regs., Part II. and the Staff Manual respectively. Title pages will be prepared in manuscript.

Place	Date	Hour	Summary of Events and Information	Remarks and references to Appendices
FIELD	9th	—	The Divn Commander woke the Division the eve of luck & hope and they he have privilege of commander including it in his command. (Sgd.) J. Burnett Stuart, Brig. Gen. G.S.C. VIth Corps.	
	10th		Battn. went to and billetted in [BEUVRY?]	
	11th		Battn. Marched up and went into supporting trenches by Cape Mounting Officers & NCOs for and instruction of [illegible] of rifles. Lieut. G.A. I.G. Matthews A.S.C. joined for duty vice Lt. Col. G. Mathews ACN [illegible] 6/E 165 recovered casualties into new trench W13 & CRATER N.C. & Crinding [illegible] very dark night. At 5am HOOD went to [illegible] by [illegible] [illegible] under 2nd Lt A.E. Cripten.	
			by evening The Jacob Manual Commander in Chief were anxiously [illegible] at 7 PM the King accompanied [illegible] to the [illegible] officers.	

WAR DIARY
or
INTELLIGENCE SUMMARY.

Army Form C. 2118.

Place	Date	Hour	Summary of Events and Information	Remarks and references to Appendices
FIELD	15th	—	Coy training	
			BAR. to MILITARY CROSS	
			LT. J.L. SMITH M.C. (2)	
			MILITARY CROSS	
			2ND LT. A.E. READ S. (2)	
	16th	—	Coy training	
			MAJOR W.H. & G. BATER M.C. Ord. AT J.L. SMITH M.C. proceed on leave	
			Coy training	
	17th	—	2ND LT. B. REDMOND reported for duties from reserve form in charge of Battn.	
			attached to 'B' Coy for duty	
			BATTN relieved 6th RN. LEICESTER REGT 2nd in sub-sector	
			H.Q. & G.M. running 6. R. relieved from sub.	
	18th	—	2ND LT. C.W. HOOD assuming command of 8 Coy vice CAPT. CLIFORD	
			116 L. CAPT. MULLALY (Acting)	
			Quiet day in the line with exception of some activity by enemy	
			with Trench Mortars.	
	19th	—	No. 61873 PTE EDWARDS.C & "C" Coy WOUNDED	

Army Form C. 2118.

WAR DIARY
or
INTELLIGENCE SUMMARY.
(Erase heading not required.)

Place	Date	Hour	Summary of Events and Information	Remarks and references to Appendices
FIELD	20th	—	No. 11873 PTE. EDWARDS, C. "C" COY. DIED OF WOUNDS.	
"	21st	—	LT/QMT. M. SYLVESTER and 2nd LT. S.R. ROBINSON joined on leave.	LT.Q.M.R. attached
"	22nd	—	Batn. relieved by 1st King's R. and shared with Brigade Support	
"	23rd	—	No. 27124 PTE. BURKBY, R. "A" COY. WOUNDED.	
"	24th	—	2nd LT. H.E. READ, M.C. rejoined "A" COY	
"	25th	—	No. 36154 PTE. JACKSON, C. "B" COY. WOUNDED.	
"	26th	—	Quiet day	
"	27th	—	Bn. relieved by 2nd Bn. ROYAL DUBLIN FUSILIERS and moved back to H.Qrs. Camp. BEUVRY.	2nd LT. N.B.S. attached
"	28th	—	Bn. moved back to DAINVILLE by bus + billeted there	2nd LT. N.B.S. attached
"	29th	—	Bn. cleaning up. Inspection of men + kit by the C.R. by the Commanding Officer. MAJOR W.H.C. GOATER, M.C. (from Leave) rejoined (resumed) the duties as 2nd Bn. Commander. vice CAPT. G.A. TURNER.	
"	30th		CAPT. G.A. TURNER resuming command of "B" COY vice 2nd LT. G.W. YOO.	

WAR DIARY
or
INTELLIGENCE SUMMARY.

(Erase heading not required.)

Army Form C. 2118.

Place	Date	Hour	Summary of Events and Information	Remarks and references to Appendices
FIELD	29th	—	CAPT. E.B. PARKER assumed command of 10th Coy. vice CAPT. P.W.E. THOMSON	
"	30th	—	2nd LT. W.D. CHAMBERLAIN proceeded to England (sick) & attack of Influenza of the Coy. 0/c 29/8/17 Battn. Bathing	
"	31st	—	Company training	

31/8/17

D.H.L. North Major
10th Bn. Yorkshire Regiment

Army Form C. 2118.

WAR DIARY
or
INTELLIGENCE SUMMARY.
(Erase heading not required.)

104th Inf Rgt 62
25 B.
5 sheets

Place	Date	Hour	Summary of Events and Information	Remarks and references to Appendices
FIELD	1st	—	Special Company training. Commenced preliminary with attack on M—	
	2nd	—	we limited objective. Attack on rifles on every 2 days interval.	
	3rd	—	Church parade.	
		—	Battalion Route March.	
	4th	—	Company training. LT. F.G. ALEXANDER proceeded to commence training +	
		—	struck off strength of Battalion.	
		—	LT. F. PEPPER assumed duties as B.n Signalling Officer.	
	5th	—	Company training.	
	6th	—	Company training. LT. E. PEPPER proceeded on leave to the REND	
		—	proceed. Duties as B.n S.O. during his absence in being	
	7th	—	Company training	
	8th	—	D2J	
	9th	—	Church Parade. After Church Parade the C.O.C. Brg. General	
		—	presented medals ribbons to the following:—	

WAR DIARY or INTELLIGENCE SUMMARY

Army Form C. 2118.

Place	Date	Hour	Summary of Events and Information	Remarks and references to Appendices
FIELD	9th	—	2nd Lt. H.E. READ – "C" Coy. — No 12047 SERGT E.K. LANE "C" Coy — No 12948 SERGT E.W. JONES "B" Coy. — No 18979 SERGT T. O'BRIEN "D" Coy — No 17592 SERGT T. HIRST "C" Coy — No 23285 CPL. A. DYKES "C" Coy — No 3898 L. CPL. F. RAINE "C" Coy — No 32043 PTE G.H. HOWEL "D" Coy 2nd Lt E.R. JAMES (these) proceeded on leave. Brigade sports took place at WAGENRIED (MAP SH 51)	
	10th	—	Company training. First round given by the newly formed B.n. Lewis Party (THE MINNIES) for representation of Pte. & nd Army of the Relicion "annual" in Faine. Extract from London Gazette:- 2nd Lt. J.T.C. STORY to be Capt. (additional) 2/39th July 1917	
	11th		Brigade Sports took place at WAGENRIED.	
	12th		Company training "D" Coy.	
	13th		Night operations. Extract from London Gazette:- TEMP 2nd LT. A.W. BIRD to be TEMP LIEUT. 2/9th May 1917.	

Army Form C. 2118.

WAR DIARY
or
INTELLIGENCE SUMMARY.

(Erase heading not required.)

Place	Date	Hour	Summary of Events and Information	Remarks and references to Appendices
FIELD	14th	—	Battalion practised new formation for the attack. CAPT. J R SHORT proceeded on leave.	
"	15	—	Bn formed up in new attacking tape in Bde practice of new attack formation.	
"	16	—	Church parade. Bn marched to and entrained at SAILLY (MAP SH 9C) & was sent to L'HESTRE (MAP SH.HAZEBROUCK 5A) at 2.28am on the 17.	N⁰ 85 SH HAZEBROUCK 5A
"	17	—	Marched to and billetted at BORRE (MAP SH.HAZEBROUCK 5F). 2nd Lt. R. SPEIGHT reports his arrival & taken on strength of Bn. posted to "A" Coy for duty.	
"	18	—	Parade under Company arrangements	
"	19	—	Practice of new formation for attack in conjunction with other coy lines.	
"	20	—	Bn Route March. LT. S. KONIG proceeded on leave. LT.E.PEPPER returned from leave	
"	21	—	Company training.	
"	22	—	Ditto	

WAR DIARY
or
INTELLIGENCE SUMMARY.

Army Form C. 2118.

Place	Date	Hour	Summary of Events and Information	Remarks and references to Appendices
FIELD	23rd	—	Bn. marched to and arrived at LA ROUGEVILLE and (Maj. Sh. HAZEBROUCK) attached.	Sc. 00 N2 63
"	24th	—	2nd Lt. H.E. READ M.O. proceeded on leave. Company training. Bn. practice of new formation for attack. 2nd Lt. R.A. JAMES returned from leave. Joined the 9th grade C.R.O. No 1635 for the following Officers C.R.O. (the budges of rank of 2/Lt. having completed 18 months service.) — 2nd Lt. O. GREENWOOD 2nd Lt. A.C. GRIFFEN 2nd Lt. S.R. DOBINSON 2nd Lt. C. DAVISON 2nd Lt. H.E. READ. 2nd Lt. C.H. PERKINS 2nd Lt. H. HUME 2nd Lt. A. DICKINSON 2nd Lt. G.S. BARTON	
"	25th	—	Company training + Bn. practice of new attack formation.	
"	26th	—	Bn. practice of new attack formation in morning (good linear attack). Bathing during afternoon of coy. The following Officers having proceeded to Eng. (ast/9AFC) coy rank of 2nd Lt. giving up rank. — Capt. K.I. COLLINS Lt. J.K. SMITH. M.G.	

Army Form C. 2118.

WAR DIARY
or
INTELLIGENCE SUMMARY.

(Erase heading not required.)

Instructions regarding War Diaries and Intelligence Summaries are contained in F. S. Regs., Part II. and the Staff Manual respectively. Title pages will be prepared in manuscript.

No. 5

Place	Date	Hour	Summary of Events and Information	Remarks and references to Appendices
FIELD	27th	—	Company training.	See O.O. No 69 attached.
"	28th	—	Bn. marched to and bivouaced at YORK CAMP. CAPT J.R. SHORT returned from leave. (M.O. 29).	
"	29th	—	Company training.	
"	30th	—	Church parade. CAPT F.R. PARKER proceeded on leave.	

12 – 10 – 17

W. H. G. Gower Major
10th Bn. Yorkshire Regt

10 YORKSHIRE REGT
62/21

Army Form C. 2118.

WAR DIARY
or
INTELLIGENCE SUMMARY.
(Erase heading not required.)

Summary of Events and Information OCTOBER 1917

Place	Date	Hour	Summary of Events and Information	Remarks and references to Appendices
			Total Strength of Bn. on 1st Oct. 37 OFF. 966 O.R.	
			Fighting Strength of Bn. on 1st Oct. 30 OFF. 897 O.R.	
FIELD	1st	3p.m.	Battalion marched to and encamped in No 2 AREA "H" CAMP	Map. SH. 28. N.W. Sec. B.O. No 69 alt 2 APPENDIX. E.
			at 4.35. C. 70. 40. map DICKEBUSCH LAKE.	
	2nd	5p.m.	After a comfortable night the Battalion marched to and	Map SH. 28. A B.O. N°69.70 APPENDIX. E
			bivouaced at ZILLEBEKE LAKE when 500 O.R. were taken	
			by shells which fell among A Coy. Others were saved by the	
			The 21st Div. was about to take part in an attack by the	Map. Sh. GHELUVELT 1/10,000 O.N°69B. APPENDIX. E.
			2nd Army on the high ground REUTEL - NOORDEMDHOEK -	
			MOLENAARELSTHOEK - NIEWE - MOLEN. The objective of the Bn.	
			being the line J. 12. d. @ 10.55 ⚹ - J. 11. b. 95. 15.	
			The following were the Senior Officers with the Bn:-	
			LT. COL. T.G. MATHIAS. D.S.O. Commanding.	
			MAJOR W.H.G. GOATER. M.C. 2nd in C.	
			CAPT. + ADJT. M. BASS.	
			CAPT. J.C. STORY. Comdg A. COY.	

WAR DIARY or INTELLIGENCE SUMMARY

Army Form C. 2118.

Place	Date	Hour	Summary of Events and Information	Remarks and references to Appendices
FIELD	3rd	—	Capt. G.A. TURNER. Comdg 'B' COY.	
"			Capt. C.H. ADWICK. Comdg 'C' COY.	
"			Capt. A.W.I. THOMSON. Comdg 'D' COY.	
"		9 p.m.	After all necessary equipment (Lewis, ammunition etc) had been issued, the Battalion left ZILLEBEKE LAKE, by platoons, 'D' Coy leading followed by 'B' Coy – 'C' Coy & 'A' Coy and the leading platoon reached CLAPHAM JUNCTION (J.13.a.95.80.) at 12 mid-nt. and met the Commanding Officer, who had pushed the Bn. fwd reconnaissance parties (1 x the C.O.) decided to take up 'B' & 'D' Coys (front line Coys) bivouac bis. The jumping off point, following & keeping in touch with the two front line Coys of the 12/13. NORTHUMBERLAND FUS, and that 'A' & 'C' Coys & H.Q. wd) follow the last supporting Battn. Coys of the same unit (12/13 N.F.) which wd pass CLAPHAM JUNCTION at 1.30 a.m. (4th).	Map. Sh. 28
"	4th	—	On arriving at GLENCORSE WOOD (J.14.a.&.b.) 'B' & 'D' Coys came under	Map Sh 28.

Army Form C. 2118.

WAR DIARY
or
INTELLIGENCE SUMMARY.
(Erase heading not required.)

3

Place	Date	Hour	Summary of Events and Information	Remarks and references to Appendices
FIELD	4th		a heavy hostile barrage and as a result each Bn 12th/13th N.F. was lost.	
	"	1.30 am	A & C Coys & H.Q left CLAPHAM JUNCTION behind the 12th/13th N.F. and also came under the heavy hostile barrage at GLENCORSE WOOD, but in spite of this touch was maintained forward	Map. Sh. 28
			BLACK WATCH CORNER (J.15.a.60.80.) was reached at 2.30 am. but here again another heavy barrage was encountered & an order was given to take shelter in shell-holes. Meanwhile touch was lost with the 12/13 N.F. & the whole Bn. was at this junction in the vicinity of BLACK WATCH CORNER under heavy shell fire without guides, & the task of regaining touch proved a very formidable one. Eventually the Bn. succeeded in jumping off from at 5.15 am to find the 1st/13th LINCOLNSHIRE REGT. occupying the position which the Bn. was to have taken. The C.O. of 1st/4th LIN. R. appreciating the situation, & realizing the dangerous position of the Bn. at BLACK WATCH CORNER in the barrage, which he overcame	

Army Form C. 2118.

WAR DIARY
or
INTELLIGENCE SUMMARY.
(Erase heading not required.)

Place	Date	Hour	Summary of Events and Information	Remarks and references to Appendices
FIELD	4th	—	would prevent it from getting into position (3 a.m. 6 a.m.) and his Bn. dispd. into position on the left of 12/13 N.F. and so the Bn. (10th YORK. R.) became rear Bn. on a two [?] just in front of POLYGONE WOOD (S.10.A+C.)	Map Sh. 28
	"	6am	At 6am an intense barrage was put down by the enemy, in the area in front of POLYGONE WOOD. During the period 9 p.m. on 3rd to 6 am on 4th the Bn. had suffered heavy losses from shell fire, but in spite of this the morale of all ranks remained high. During the day the hostile artillery fire continued unceasingly.	
	"	3pm	An S.O.S. was put up by the troops on the right & the Bn. was ready to counter-attack if necessary, but no hostile counter attack matured. Under cover of darkness the Bn. moved forward to a new position near the old front line in JUNIPER TR (J.10.6.) and consolidated there.	Map Sh. 28 1st Map Manual 7

A6945 Wt. W14472/M1160 350,000 12/16 D. D. & L. Forms/C./2118/14

Army Form C. 2118.

WAR DIARY
~~INTELLIGENCE~~ SUMMARY.
(Erase heading not required.)

5

Place	Date	Hour	Summary of Events and Information	Remarks and references to Appendices
FIELD	5th	4am	A heavy hostile barrage was put down on a line between our front line and POLYGONE WOOD.	
		7am	Artillery activity considerably quietened down, but soon after 10 a.m. enemy commenced his usual harassing fire on forward, intermediate & back area. At 4 p.m. the Commanding Officer was had been badly shaken during his efforts to an round action that he was to man back to the Nucleus Party. The previous day, when the Bn. was caught in the barrage.	
			The night 5/6th passed without event. An S.O.S. was put up in the front of the DIV on the left but no one attack matured.	
	6th	10am	MAJOR. W.H.G. COATER. M.C. repaired and assumed command of the Battalion. Hostile harassing fire continued during the whole day & two barrages were put down in answer to our particular barrage shots.	

A6945 Wt. W14424/M1160 350,000 12/16 D. D. & L. Forms/C./2118/14.

Army Form C. 2118.

WAR DIARY
or
INTELLIGENCE SUMMARY.
(Erase heading not required.)

Instructions regarding War Diaries and Intelligence Summaries are contained in F.S. Regs., Part II. and the Staff Manual respectively. Title pages will be prepared in manuscript.

Place	Date	Hour	Summary of Events and Information	Remarks and references to Appendices
FIELD	7th	—	Night passed without incident. Have morning barrage taken & been. Numerous casualties suffered by Bn. whilst having the plans launched, in which the conditions were very bad as men were advancing in a foot of mud and rain and the rest of which guns were rendered extremely difficult owing to the badly cut-up state of the ground, rendered in parts impassable after several heavy shower during the preceding day & night. Artillery activity increased in intensity as the day wore on.	
	7th	1·45 p.m.	Bn. was relieved by the 8/9th Bn. Lincoln Regt. and moved back to and bivouaced at ZILLEBEKE LAKE.	Map.Sh. 28.N.W. I.21.6.20.20.19. & 22. 2.13.09. 1/20,000.
			The Bn. lost heavily in Officers & men in this engagement. The Total casualties being 1 Off. + 7th + 74 O.R. killed and 9 Offrs. + 249 O.R. wounded & missing. The character of all ranks throughout the engagement was of the steadiest & this — The BATTLE OF THE BROODSEINDE RIDGE — proved to have resulted in a great	See APPENDIX "B"

A6945 Wt. W14422/M1160 350,000 12/16 D.D. & L. Forms/C./2118/14.

Army Form C. 2118.

WAR DIARY
~~INTELLIGENCE SUMMARY~~
(Erase heading not required.)

Place	Date	Hour	Summary of Events and Information	Remarks and references to Appendices
FIELD	7th	—	Success.	
"	8th	—	Battalion remained in bivouac resting.	APPENDIX "E" B.O. No. 71 (attached)
"	9th	11 a.m.	Battalion left ZILLEBEKE LAKE and marched by Companies to OUDERDOM STATION (6.30.a.90.00.). The C.O. & nucleus party joined Bn here and Junior (a/c.) commanded from MAJOR W.H.G. COSTER M.C. who re-assumed duties as 2nd in Command. The entrainment took place at 5 p.m. & train left at 6 p.m. (approx).	Map Sh. 26.
"	10th	1 a.m.	Detrained at EBLINGHEM STATION (T.23.6.90.30.) and marched to and billeted at SERCUS (C.19.)	Map Sh. 27. Map Sh. 36A
BILLETS	10th to 20th	—	This period was spent in general re-organisation of the Bn., a certain amount of Light training & training of Specialists being done. Inter Coy football matches were arranged & played & generally the Bn greatly benefited by the change of rest.	

Army Form C. 2118.

WAR DIARY
or
~~INTELLIGENCE SUMMARY~~

(Erase heading not required.)

Instructions regarding War Diaries and Intelligence Summaries are contained in F. S. Regs., Part II. and the Staff Manual respectively. Title pages will be prepared in manuscript.

Place	Date	Hour	Summary of Events and Information	Remarks and references to Appendices
BILLETS SERCUS	10th to 20th		ADMINISTRATIVE	
	10th		MAJOR. W. GIBBS having reported his arrival is taken on the strength of the Bn. & posted to 'A' Coy for Administration & assumes duties as 2nd in Command. (14/10/17)	
	11th		(a) MAJOR. W.H.G. FOATER. M.C. assumes command of 'C' Coy vice CAPT. C.H. ADWICK.	
			(b) CAPT. C.H. ADWICK assumes command of 'B' Coy vice CAPT. G.H. TURNER (wounded)	
			(c) LT. A.E. GRIFFEN assumes command of 'B' Coy vice CAPT. C.H. ADWICK (sick)	
	12th		(a) Ex. from Lond. Gazette:- 2nd LT. C.W. HOOD to be Acting Capt. (additional.)	
			(b) 2nd LT. C.W. HOOD relinquishes rank of Acting Capt. on proceeding to England (sick.)	
	13th		Ex. from Lond. Gazette:- Temp. 2nd Lieuts. to be Lieuts:- 2nd Lieuts. O. Greenwood - G.E. Griffin - C.W. Perkins - S.R. Adamson - H. Hunn - H.E. Read M.C. - H.V.B. DOVE. G.S. SArsun (July 20th) - A. Dickinson (July 20th)	

Army Form C. 2118.

WAR DIARY
or
INTELLIGENCE SUMMARY.
(Erase heading not required.)

9

Place	Date	Hour	Summary of Events and Information	Remarks and references to Appendices
BILLETS SEREUS	10th To 20th	—	ADMINISTRATIVE (CONT?)	

16th 2ND LT. A.F. JACOBS reported his arrival for duty and is taken on the strength & posted to 'C' Coy.

a/ CAPT. J.C. STORY relinquishes his acting rank on proceeding to England (sick.) 4-10-17.

18th (a) 2ND LT. L. MARTIN proceeded on leave.

(b) 2ND LT. T.A. HYSLOP to 2nd Army Sniping School.

(c) LT. G.S. SARSON. to 10th Corps Lewis Gun School.

(d) 2ND LT. C.W. HOOD granted 3 weeks S.L. by M.B. at Etaples.

(e) MAJOR. W. GIBBS takes on command of the Bn. vice Lt. Col. J.G. Mathias. D.S.O. (on leave).

(f) MAJOR. W.H.G. COATER. M.C. re-assumes duties as 2nd in Command vice MAJOR. W. GIBBS.

(g) LT. H.E. READ. M.C. takes on command of 'C' Coy vice MAJOR. W.H.G. COATER. M.C.

(h) 2ND LT. C.A. BOWKER takes on command of 'B' Coy vice LT. A.E. GRIFFIN (I.O.)

Army Form C. 2118.

WAR DIARY
or
INTELLIGENCE SUMMARY.
(Erase heading not required.)

Instructions regarding War Diaries and Intelligence Summaries are contained in F.S. Regs., Part II. and the Staff Manual respectively. Title pages will be prepared in manuscript.

Place	Date	Hour	Summary of Events and Information	Remarks and references to Appendices
BILLETS SERCUS	10th To 20th	—	ADMINISTRATIVE (CONT'D) (J) LT. A.E. GRIFFEN Takes over duties of Intelligence Officer vice LT. H.W. BIRD to England (wounded.)	
			19th MAJOR. W. GIBBS assumes the rank of LT. Col. on taking on command of the Bn.	O. No. 72/75 attached APPENDIX "E"
FIELD	20th	4.35 p.m.	Bn. left SERCUS and marched to EBLINGHEM STATION and entrained for DICKEBUSCH, where it arrived at 1 a.m. & marched to encamped in MICMAC CAMP (H.31.d.) at 2 a.m.	Map. 57.20 Map. 5K. 2F.
	21st			
		4.15 p.m.	Bn. left MICMAC CAMP and moved to 'C' Camp (H.20.C.) where it encamped	O. H. 274 attached. APPENDIX "E"
	22nd	9.45 a.m.	Bn. left 'C' Camp and marched by Companies to ZILLEBEKE LAKE TRONVIAC (I.15.d. 20.80 to I.21.G. 10.50.) where dinners and sub equipment (bombs etc) were issued.	O. No. 70 attached APPENDIX "E" Map. 5H. 5B
		3 p.m.	Bn. moved up to front line by platoons and relieved 8th Bn. YORK AND LANCASTER REGT. (Major Barlow D.S.O., M.C.) in the right sub-sector. Relief was completed at 9 p.m. without casualties.	O. No 75 attached APPENDIX "E"

WAR DIARY
or
INTELLIGENCE SUMMARY.
(Erase heading not required.)

Army Form C. 2118.

Place	Date	Hour	Summary of Events and Information	Remarks and references to Appendices
FIELD	22nd	—	The dispositions of the Bn. were as follows:— 'A' Coy Right Front Line (J.6.C.20.20.10.J.12.A.20.8) 'D' Coy Left Front Line 'B' Coy Left Support : 'C' Coy Right Support (J.11.A.65.95 – J.11.A.60.70. 2nd LT. A.F. JACOBS wounded (S.S.) — J.11.A.70.50.) Enemy artillery active during the night, but in spite of our front being actively patrolled no enemy was encountered.	See Appendices A2 attached.
	23rd	6am.	Enemy low flying aeroplanes active on our front line & as a result our front & support trenches were heavily shelled during the morning causing numerous casualties.	
		7p.m.	Three prisoners were taken by 'D' Coy belonging to the 36th Div, and they proved to have provided a valuable identification.	
	24th	—	Enemy artillery active throughout the day. The condition of the trenches was extremely bad. There being several heavy downpours of rain; as the subsoil was scarcely the water drained away fairly well, but the slightest concussion shook down the sides of trenches. Two enemy Taranges were put down in reply to two of our	

WAR DIARY
or
INTELLIGENCE SUMMARY.

(Erase heading not required.)

Army Form C. 2118.

Place	Date	Hour	Summary of Events and Information	Remarks and references to Appendices
FIELD	24th	—	Position Garages.	
	25th	—	Enemy shelling heavy at intervals throughout the day. Our support line received most of a great part of the shelling as it was under observation from POLDERHOEK CHATEAU (J.16.d.30.20.) which was still in enemy hands.	Map SK. 28.
	26th	6 a.m.	Enemy two flying planes active. Very heavy enemy barrage put down at "Zero" of an attack by the Canadians on the left and the 7th DIV. on the right.	
		9 p.m.	Bn. relieved by 1st BN. LINCOLNSHIRE REGT. and moved back into the ZIllEBEKE LAKE bivouac vacated on 22nd inst. Casualties 13 O.R. killed 1 Off. + 40 O.R. wounded.	See APPENDIX "O"
	27th 30th	—	Bn. resting at ZIllEBEKE LAKE in Bde. Reserve. 'B' Coy moved up + relieved a Coy of 3/4 "Queens" R.W.S. Regt. at THE BUTTE on the 29th. Bn. relieved by 15th D.L.I. + moved back to 'B' Camp.(H.20.a)	See O.N.º 75 See APPENDIX 13

ADMINISTRATIVE

232 The following Officers reported their arrival, taken on strength + posted to Companies for duty as shewn against their names:—

Army Form C. 2118

WAR DIARY
or
INTELLIGENCE SUMMARY
(Erase heading not required.)

13

Place	Date	Hour	Summary of Events and Information	Remarks and references to Appendices
FIELD	—	—	ADMINISTRATIVE (CONT^D) 2ND LT. C.F. JAMESON 'B' COY 2ND LT. A. LEE 'C' COY 2ND LT. J.D. SMITH 'D' COY 29th The Corps Commander awarded the Military Medal to the undermentioned N.C.O's & men of the Bn. No 13498 CPL. E.H. LAWS. 'A' COY No 14970 PTE. J. MIKES. 'C' COY No 36059 PTE. J. SWIFT. 'C' COY No 20407 PTE. J. GILLAN. 'A' COY No 33199 L.CPL. F. ALLISON 'C' COY No 19183. SERGT. O.M. J. BOURNES. 'D' COY The Divisional & Bde. Commanders and staffs & commanding officers & officers & other ranks of the Bn. offered their congratulations to the recipients. Total Strength of Bn. on 31st Oct. 36 OFF 589 O.R. Fighting Strength of Bn. on 31st Oct. 21 OFF 520 O.R. Field. 31/10/17 W.H.L. Foster. Major. 10th Bn. Yorkshire Regt.	See Appendices marked 'C' attached.
	31st	—		

Confidential

6/71

Army Form C. 2118.

WAR DIARY
or
INTELLIGENCE SUMMARY.

(Erase heading not required.)

10th Yorkshire Regt

November 1917

WAR DIARY
or
INTELLIGENCE SUMMARY.

(Erase heading not required.)

Army Form C. 2118.

November 1917

Place	Date	Hour	Summary of Events and Information	Remarks and references to Appendices
YPRES AREA	1st		Bn in "B" Camp at CHATEAU SEGARD. Resting after tour in line.	
	2nd		CHATEAU SEGARD. Resting.	
	3rd		Bn move to Railway dug-outs ZILLEBEKE LAKE	App A
	4th		Bn take up line of Trenches 1500° East of POLYGONE BUTTE, 2 Companies front line & 2 in Support. H.Q at POLYGONE BUTTE.	Apps B & C
	5th		Relief completed 12.15 a.m. Heavy shelling intermittently	
	6th		Our Trenches & back areas heavily shelled, mostly on account of our attacks this date on PASCHENDAELE & just south of us on POLDERHOEK CHATEAU	
	7th		Shelling heavy on back areas	
	8th		Bn relieved by 7/8th div. coys. A.B.& D. Coys move to CLAPHAM JUNCTION & T.H.Q. C. Coy to ZILLEBEKE LAKE. O.R. in Support	Apps D & E
	9th		Working parties provided from CLAPHAM JUNCTION	
	10		CLAPHAM JUNCTION. Heavy shelling.	
	11		Bn relieved by 1st Bedford R.E. & move to MICMAC CAMP	App F

WAR DIARY
INTELLIGENCE SUMMARY

Army Form C. 2118.

November 1917

Place	Date	Hour	Summary of Events and Information	Remarks and references to Appendices
YPRES and	11		Casualties from Nov 16th to 11th shown in —	App F(a)
	12		MICMAC CAMP. Men resting after very arduous tour in line. Re-equipment commenced	
			2/Lts. Bloom, Morris, Cliffe, Arundel & Wray joined	
	13		MICMAC Camp	
	14		MICMAC Camp	
	15		Bn marched to "H" Camp WESTOUTRE (M.9.a.5.8)	App. G
	16		At WESTOUTRE	
	17		Bn marched VIEUX BERQUIN & billeted in farms	App. H
	18		Bn marched to VEDDIN PRES-BETHUNE & billeted - & brigade trench & inspection en route by G.O.C 5 Division & Bgde.	" J
	19		Bn marched to HERSIN & accommodated there in Adrian huts	App K
	20		To MONT ST ELOY & accommodated in OTTAWA Camp	App L
	21		To ECURIE - B" in WAKEFIELD Camp	" M
	22		At ECURIE Major R Howlett D.S.O, MC arrived and took	" N

WAR DIARY
or
INTELLIGENCE SUMMARY.

Army Form C. 2118.

November 1917

Place	Date	Hour	Summary of Events and Information	Remarks and references to Appendices
AREAS as at	22		On Command of the battalion was at Lt. Col. W. Gibbs 10th Hussars the latter assuming 2nd in command.	
	23		At Ecurie.	
	24		At Ecurie. Lt. Southlands 2nd Lt. Crapper, Coker & Morrison joined the battalion. Training continued.	
	25		Churches on OPPY front visited & perhaps by relieving army. App.O. Bath errand visited by Officers & "continuing"	
	26			
	27		Training at ECURIE	
	28			
	29			
	30		Bn. entrained at MAROEUIL & arrived at PERONNE STN. & arrived at BRUSLE camp on Dec 1st	

W. Fitt Major
10th Yorkshire Regt.

"10" York & Lanc Regt A SECRET.

Map INELUVELT.   Order No. 6   2 - 11 - 17

1. 62 Inf.y Bde. will relieve 110 Inf. Bde. between Nov 3rd & 5th in the right in the right sector of Divisional front. 15th York R. will relieve 9th Leicester R in the Left Sub Sector on the night of 4/5th.

2. 10th York R. will relieve 9th Leicester Regt in Reserve in Railway dugouts tomorrow 3rd inst.

3. Batt will move by Coys. at 200 yards interval, 1st Coy. leaving B Camp at 2.30 p.m. tomorrow 3rd inst. Order of march. H. B. C. D. Coys. H.R.

4. Lieut Loney will remain with Nucleus party and Lieut Dobinson will take charge of carrying party. Lieut Dobinson will arrange to take over RAILWAY DUGOUTS from the 9th Leicester Regt. at 1.30 pm tomorrow. 1 N.C.O per Coy and H.Q. will meet him at H.Q. 9th Leicester R. at 1.30 pm tomorrow.

5. Officers Kits & Orderly Room stores will be collected at 1.30 pm and taken to RAILWAY DUGOUTS. Mess Baskets will be collected at 2 pm and also taken to RAILWAY DUGOUTS.
   Blankets will be rolled in bundles of 10, collected at 1.30 pm & taken to 97 DUGOUTS. Each Company will detail its own loading party.

6. 1 Officer, 1 N.C.O & 2 Runners per Coy. will proceed to H.Q. 8 Leicester R. at the BUTTE DE POLYGON leaving companys at 8 am on morning 8 4th.

7. Carrying party under Lieut Dobinson will remain behind in RAILWAY DUGOUTS when the Batt. moves off on the 4th.

8. Companies will take over the line as follows:-
   B. Coy - Right Front Line Company
   C " - Left " " "
   A " - Right Support "
   D " - Left " "

9. Cookers & Mallese cart will accompany the Batt to RAILWAY DUGOUTS.

10. When Battn moves off on 4th each man will carry 2 days rations in addition to Iron Rations. These will be issued on morning of 4th. An extra 50 rounds S.A.A. per man will be carried. Transport officer will arrange to draw same and take to RAILWAY DUGOUTS by 10 am 4th.

District 1. -
H.Q. Warapan & File
" 4.5.6 Companies
7. " "
8. " "
9. " "
   M.O.

Capt & Adjt
10th York R.

Copy No. 10th Yorkshire Regt.   B   Secret

Ref. Odements   Order No 80.   3-11-17

1. 10th York R. will relieve 8th Leicester R. in left sub sector tomorrow 4th inst.

2. B Coy. 10th York R. will relieve Right Front Line Company.
   C.   "   "   "   "   Left   "   "
   A.   "   "   "   "   Right Support Company
   D.   "   "   "   "   Left   "   "

3. Batt. will move by Companies at 200 yards interval in following order H.Q. B.C.D.A. Coys. H.Q. will leave RAILWAY DUGOUTS at 4.30 p.m.

4. Men will carry leather waistcoat (to be worn) Ground sheet, iron rations, 2 days rations + extra 50 rounds S.A.A. in haversacks. Water bottles will be filled at 2.30 p.m.

5. Blankets will be rolled in bundles of 10 + collected at 10.30 a.m. Transport Officer will make arrangements to have them brought back to Q.M. Stores. Each Coy. will arrange its own loading party.
   Packs will be dumped at RAILWAY DUGOUTS in a place to be selected by Lieut Robinson at 2 p.m. He will arrange for them to be put either under cover or to be covered by bivouac sheets.
   R.S.M. will issue S.A.A. at 10.30 a.m.

6. Officers kits will be collected at 2.30 p.m. + mess baskets + Orderly Room stores at 5 p.m.

7. Relief complete will be notified to H.Q. by runner by the word "FRANK".

8. Carrying party will bring water to the BUTTE on the morning of the 5th.

9. Grenades, Rifle Grenades + S.O.S. Rockets will be taken over on relief. Numbers taken over will be sent to H.Q. as soon as possible after relief has been reported complete. Disposition of Companies will be sent in as soon as possible after relief.

10. Following returns will be required daily
    1. Wind + situation report 4 am - 4 pm.
    2. Casualties 12 noon to 12 noon — by 12 noon.
    3. General report on activities 4 pm to 4 pm to be at H.Q. by 4.30 p.m.
    4. Indents R.E. Material, S.A.A. &c required at H.Q. by 4.30 p.m.

11. Guides for Coys. will meet Coys. at BUTTE DE POLYGON at 6.30 p.m. on 4th inst.

(Signed) H. Bass.
Captain & Adjutant
10th York R.

Nº 22 — **MESSAGE MAP.** — German Trenches corrected to 16-10-17.

Brigade Dispositions

Nº 22   MESSAGE MAP.   German Trenches corrected to 16-10-17.

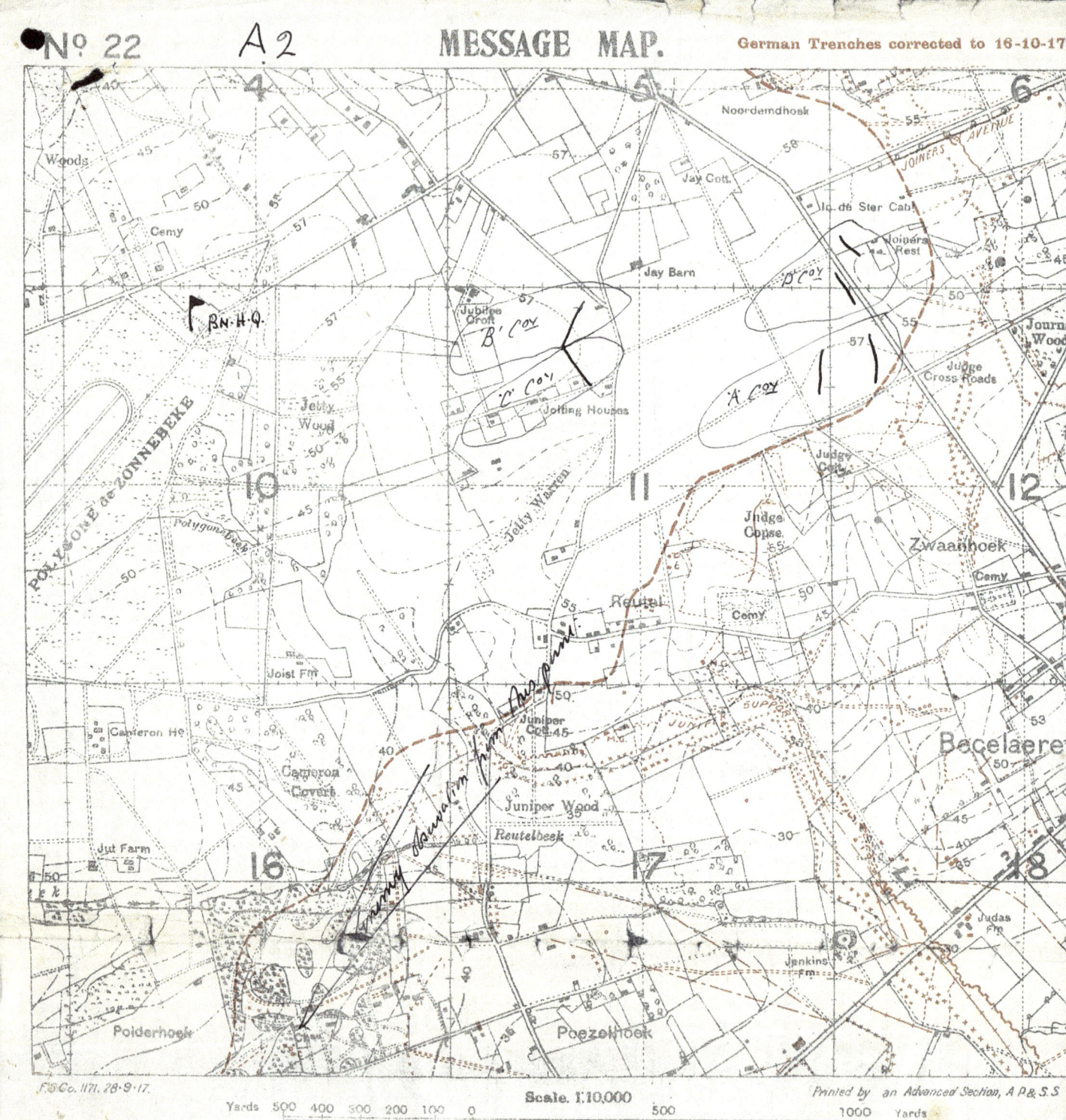

D Secret

10th Yorkshire Regiment Order No. 81

7-11-17

1. 10th York R. will be relieved by 1st Lincoln R. in left sub-sector on the night 8/9th.

2. 1st Lincoln R. will pass HOOGE CRATER at 5-45 p.m. 2 Guides per Coy from 10th York R. will be at the BUTTE at 6.30 p.m. tomorrow. Each guide will be given a note stating what guide he is i.e. RIGHT FRONT LINE COY etc.

3. 1 Officer 1 NCO + 2 runners per Coy of 1st Lincoln R. will report to Batt. H.Q. about 8 am tomorrow + will be sent up to Coys.

4. All grenades, rifle grenades, S.O.S. signals, Lewis Gun magazines, maps etc. will be handed over on relief.

5. Completion of relief of Front + Support Lines will be notified by the word "GEORGE".

6. On relief "A" Coy will move to support to Right Batt. 12/13 NF in MEBUS in JETTYWOOD. O.C. A Coy will arrange to reconnoitre position during day.

On relief B + C Coys. will move to dugouts at CLAPHAM JUNCTION. Guide to CLAPHAM JUNCTION found by 12/13 NF will meet Coys at the BUTTE.

D Coy will move back to the BUTTE to dugouts in the side of it.

All Coys will take over L.G. Magazines from 12/13 Northd. Fus.

7. Major Goater MC. will arrange to send men to CLAPHAM JUNCTION on the afternoon of the 8th to prepare for the two Coys. there with regard to hot tea + dry socks.

He will also arrange to send direct to the BUTTE for D Coy. on the 8th.

(Signed) H. Pass
Capt & Adjt
10th York R.

Amendment to 18th Yorkshire Order No 81.

1. Ref. Para 6 cancelled.
   On relief A.B.C. Coys will move back to CLAPHAM JUNCTION. Guides will meet Coys at the BUTTE as Coys move out.
   On relief D. Coy will move to RAILWAY DUGOUTS, ZILLEBEKE where accommodation will be arranged by Staff Captain 63rd Inf. Brigade.

2. Major W.H. Coates M.C. will make necessary arrangements for receiving the Bat. in the new dispositions.

Copy No 1.   SECRET
                                                                        9.11.17

10th E. Yorkshire Regiment
Defence Scheme Support Battalion.

1. 62nd Inf Bde holds the Right Sector of Divisional Front - boundaries of Front line J10d.90.10 — J.12a.20.30
Bde has Two battalions in Front line - One Bn in Support (with 3 Coys at CLAPHAM JUNCTION and 1 Coy at RAILWAY DUGOUTS - ZILLEBEKE and 1 Batt in Reserve in RAILWAY DUGOUTS ZILLEBEKE.

2. In case of Alarm the Support Battn will at once "Stand to Arms" and await orders.

3. Action of Support Battalion in case of hostile attack.
(a) On receipt of information that the two Counter attack Coys at the BUTTE and MEBUS at J10d.00.50 having moved forward to Counter attack 'A' and 'D' Coys 10 York R will move forward and occupy the MEBUS and BUTTE respectively. On arrival each Coy will send two orderlies to HQ 12/13 North'd Fus and HQ 1st Lincoln R at the BUTTE reporting their arrival. They will come under the direct orders of OC Battn mentioned above.
(b) 'B' Coy will remain in present position and await further orders.
(c) 'C' Coy on receipt of orders will move up to CLAPHAM JUNCTION and await orders.
(d) Bn HQ will remain in present position at J13d.8.7 and move up with 'B' and 'C' Coys.

Distribution.   A Bass Appadj
Copy No 1 File   10 York R.
2.3.4.5 OC Coys
  6   12/13th North'd Fus.
  7   1st Lincoln R
  8   62nd Inf Bde

SECRET.   B.M.30/107

82nd Infantry Brigade Defence Scheme.

Ref. Map GHELUVELT 1/10.000.

1.   The 82nd Infantry Brigade holds the Right Sector of the Divisional Front.
     Brigade and Battalion boundaries and dispositions are shown on attached Map "A" (issued to those particularly concerned).

2.   The distribution of the Brigade is as follows :-

   Front Line.

   (a) Right Battalion.   —   Battn. H.Q. ~~Polygone.~~ BUTTE DE POLYGONE.
       (2 companies)   J.11.c.0.4 – J.11.c.5.4 –
                                  J.11.c.6.5 – J.11.c.9.5 –
                                  J.11.d.1.4.

   (b) Left Battalion.   —   Battn. H.Q. BUTTE DE POLYGONE.
       (2 companies)   J.11.d.4.5 – J.11.d.7.5 –
                                  J.12.c.0.9 – J.12.a.2.2 –
                                  J.12.a.5.4.

   Supports.

   (a) Right Battalion.   —   Half Company in close support
       (1 company).   to Right Company in trench
                                  from: J.11.c.1.4 – J.11.c.5.5.
                                  Half Company in trench from
                                  J.11.c.8.5 – J.11.c.9.7.

   (b) Left Battalion.   —   Trenches J.11.c.8.7 –
       (1 company).   J.11.a.9.5.

   Counter-attack companies.

   (a) Right Battalion.   —   Vicinity of BUTTE DE POLYGONE.
       (1 company).

   (b) Left Battalion.   —   (In Mebus in vicinity of
       (1 company).   ~~J.10.d.~~ J.10.c.9.6.)

   Support Battalion.   —   Battn. H.Q. Mebus at
       (less 2 companies).   J.12.d.8.7.
                                  2 companies in the TUNNEL at
                                  CLAPHAM JUNCTION.

   2 Companies.   —   ZILLEBEKE.

   Brigade Reserve.

       1 Battalion.   —   Railway Dugouts, ZILLEBEKE.

   Machine Gun Coy.   —   H.Q. J.10.b.1.7.
                                12 guns in Forward Area.
                                 4 guns in Reserve.

   Trench Mortar Battery. —   Not in line.

   Brigade H.Q.   —   HOOGE CRATER.

3. In case of alarm:

   (a) Officers Commanding Battalions will inform Bde. H.Q. at once by the quickest means available.

   (b) All troops of the Brigade will stand to arms.

   (c) The Reserve Battalion will send an officer to Bde. H.Q. as soon as possible and will report immediately they are ready to move off.

4. Offensive Action by the enemy.

   Should an attack develop anywhere against the Divisional Front, the most probable points on which it would be directed appear to be :-

   (a) With a limited objective against the IN DE STER CABARET and high ground just North of JUDGE COTTAGE, so as to obtain observation.

   (b) Between REUTEL and JUDGE COTTAGE with the object of regaining the Plateau (Northern 'J' squares). Enemy troops intended for this attack would probably assemble in the South-western outskirts of BECELAERE.

5. Action of Front Line and Support Battalions in case of hostile attack.

   (a) The General line of the REUTEL - JAY BARN - J.8 central road forms the Support line of the Divisional Sector and must be held to the last.

   (b) Should the enemy penetrate our front line he will immediately be counter-attacked by the counter-attacking companies and the line re-established.

   (c) One company from each battalion is to be employed solely as counter-attack companies. These counter-attack companies are to be entirely separate from the troops detailed to act as garrisons to the various defences.
   Orders will be given to both O.C. Companies that they are to deliver counter-attacks on their own initiative on any portion of the Brigade front without awaiting instructions, should the situation demand it. It is of the utmost importance that they should know all the ground over which they may have to act.

   (d) It should be remembered that a counter-attack delivered against the flanks of the enemy is most likely to achieve the best results.

   (e) Should the two counter-attack companies be used to make a counter-attack the 2 companies of the Support battalion at CLAPHAM JUNCTION will move up at once and occupy the positions vacated by them.

- 2 -

    (f)   Should a Battalion Commander consider that he has not sufficient troops for the defence of his line he must inform Bde. H.Q. at once.

6.   Officers and Senior N.C.Os of the Reserve Battalion should reconnoitre the routes up to the front.

7.   The 12 Machine Guns are placed so as to defend especially important points.

8.   The Brigade is covered by 94th, 95th and 82nd R.F.A. Brigades.

    The S.O.S. lines as far as this Brigade Sector is concerned are as follows :-

    J.11.d.5.1 – J.12.c.0.5 – J.12.c.35.90 – J.12.a.8.8.

    The valley South of REUTEL is covered by Machine Guns.

    There is a Senior Liaison Officer at Bde. H.Q. and a Liaison Officer at the BUTTE DE POLYGONE.

9.   The S.O.S. signal now in use is a Rifle Grenade shewing three coloured lights – RED, GREEN and YELLOW.

10.   In active operations, whether initiated by the enemy or ourselves, flares will be lit when called for by contact aeroplanes.

11.   The following appendices are attached :-

    Appendix "A".   -   Position of Machine Guns.
        " "B".   -   Communications.

    Any other appendices, which may be considered necessary, will be forwarded later.

12.   Brigade H.Q. will remain at HOOGE CRATER.

                       G.M. Sharpe.
                          Capt,
                          Bde. Major,
                          62 Infantry Bde.

8/11/17.

Distribution.

    12/13 Northd Fus.   D.A.D.O.
    1 Lincoln R.   Senior Liaison Officer.
    10 York R.   Staff Captain.
    2/4 "The Queens" (RWS) R.
    62 M.G.Coy.
    21 Division.
    9" Inf. Bde.
    110 " "

APPENDIX "A".

Position of Machine Guns.

J.11.d.70.75.
J.11.d.80.85.
J.11.c.70.50.
J.11.c.75.50.
J.11.c.20.40.
J.10.d.80.85.   A
J.10.d.75.80.
J.10.d.15.90.
J.10.d.20.95.
J.10.b.25.00.   A
J.10.b.25.00.
J.10.c.20.70.   A

A = mounted for Anti-aircraft.

APPENDIX "B".

COMMUNICATIONS.

1. Communication with both front line Battalion H.Q. situated at BUTTE at J.10.a.6.8, is as follows :-

    (a) Cable from Bde. H.Q. to G.W. J.14.a.4.4., thence by visual to BUTTE.

    (b) Cable from Bde. H.Q. to G.W. J.14.a.4.4., visual to "ZN" J.9.a.9.5, and cable or visual to BUTTE.

    (c) Wireless Bde. H.Q. to Corps Directing Station and forward to Set at J.9.b.9.2, power buzzer, visual or runner to BUTTE.

    (d) Runner posts are situated at J.8.c.4.5, J.8.b.8.5, J.9.a.9.5 and at BUTTE. Posts leave Bde. H.Q. at 6 a.m. and 3.30 p.m. and from BUTTE at 8 a.m. and 5.30 p.m.

    (e) Pigeons are supplied daily to battalions for distribution to Coys. at the rate of 2 pairs per day per Battalion.

    (f) If the line to G.W. J.14.a.4.8, is cut there is visual communication from I.18.b.1.7, near Bde. H.Q.

2. There is a speaking pair to Support Battn. H.Q. at CLAPHAM JUNCTION.

3. Reserve Battn. H.Q. are connected to Bde. by telephone, through Div. H.Q.

4. Between Bde. and Div. H.Q. there are two speaking pairs and two message circuits. There is also visual communication between Bde. and YEOMANRY POST if lines are cut.

5. Communication to Bde. on right through Div. H.Q.

F

10th Yorkshire Regiment Order No 82. 10-11-17

1. 62nd Inf Brigade will be relieved by 15th Inf Brigade + 3rd New Zealand Rifle Brigade between 11th & 12th November.
   10th York R, in support will be relieved by 12th Bedford Regt. on night 11/12.

2. C. Coy will leave RAILWAY DUGOUTS, ZILLEBEKE at 2pm 11th inst. & will march to area F/8 H (LA CLYTTE) under their own arrangements.
   Transport Officer will arrange with O.C. C. Coy time transport will be required. (Carrying party will accompany C. Coy)

3. O.C. A + D. Coys. will divide the space now occupied by A.B.D. Coys. into two Coys accommodation + will each detail 3 guides to report at HOOGE CRATER at 11.30 pm. on 11th inst. One runner for B.H.Q. will report at same time & place. O.C. A. Coy. will detail one officer to take charge of all guides.

4. As soon as first Coy 12th Bedford R arrives at CLAPHAM JUNCTION B. Coy will move off. On relief A + D. Coys. will move away first reporting relief complete by word BASIL either by telephone or runner.

5. Transport Officer will arrange for transport to be at CLAPHAM JUNCTION at 3 pm. tomorrow to remove stores.

6. On relief Coys will move via HELLFIRE CORNER – CORDUROY TRACK to SHRAPNEL CORNER – x roads H.30 d 21 x roads H 29 b 55 – LA CLYTTE.
   First halt will occur when head of column reaches a point 100 yards off SHRAPNEL CORNER where a distance of 200 yards between Coys. will be observed.

7. Major W.H.G. Goates will arrange for sending an advance party to take over camp + for hot tea to be served on arrival of men.

8. Transport, Quarter Masters stores, Nucleus party will move under their own arrangements.

9. Name of Camp at Area H will be notified later.

10. Officers chargers will meet them at x roads H. 30 c 3.8. (Transport lines)

(Signed) H Bass
Capt + Adjt.
10th York R.

Casualties – 4th to 11th November 1917

Date	Number	Rank & Name	Company	State of Casualty
5-11-17	305640	Private Sealey W.	A	Killed
5-11-17	261524	L/Cpl. Cash B.	D	"
4-11-17	126441	Private Holmes H.	B	"
6-11-17	114921	L/S.M. Garvey A.	A	"
5-11-17	64496	Private Jones W.	B	"
5-11-17	241906	" Loines E.	D	"
6-11-17	36798	" McGowan J.	A	"
6-11-17	25180	" Walland G.L.	C	"
6-11-17	305491	" Pearson A.	D	"
6-11-17	17371	L/S.M. Brown W.	D	Wounded
6-11-17	17365	Private Bradley E.	D	"
8-11-17	26286	" Blenkinsop J.	A	"
7-11-17	339415	" Chambers S. (+ Shell Shock)	B	"
5-11-17	17378	Sergt. Clark W. (Died of Wounds)	D	"
6-11-17	26685	Private Coates G.	A	"
6-11-17	114941	" Clegg J.	A	"
5-11-17	33138	" Cook F.	B	"
6-11-17	45576	" Dunn J.	D	"
6-11-17	33068	" Fowell F.	D	"
5-11-17	201852	" Foster K.	B	"
5-11-17	18016	" Guy J.	A	"
7-11-17	19085	Sergt. Griggs H.	A	"
6-11-17	27538	Private Hooper J.	C	"
6-11-17	19696	" Heaton J. (at Duty)	B	"
6-11-17	266112	" Lamb J.	C	"
5-11-17	241904	" Pruscoll (at Duty)	B	"
6-11-17	255820	" Smith W.H.	D	"
6-11-17	33222	" Smith E.	D	"
6-11-17	38059	" Swift J.	C	"
6-11-17	35221	" Smithson W.	D	"
6-11-17	114912	L/Sgt. Straight J.F.	C	"
6-11-17	201665	Private Wilford J.	D	"
7-11-17	38811	L/Sgt. Wood J.J.	B	"
5-11-17	242153	Private Webster W.	D	"
6-11-17		2/Lieut. Martin	B	"
7-11-17		2/Lieut. Jamieson (at Duty)	B	"
11-11-17	17291	Private Kean P. (at Duty)	A	"
11-11-17		2/Lieut. Speight H. (at Duty)	A	"
11-11-17		2/Lieut. Bowler G.A. (E 5-11-17)		"
13-11-17	235098	Pte. Radford F. (Accidental)	D	"

10th Bn. Yorkshire Regt.

Order B.   13th November 1917

1. 10th York R. will move by road to YORK CAMP, M.3.c.5.8 on the 15th inst.

2. Billeting party consisting of Officer, H.Qrs., Interpreter with one representative per Coy. & Batt. H.Q. on cycles, will leave at 8.30 a.m. & meet Staff Captain 62nd Inf. Bde. at Office of area commandant, WESTOUTRE at 10 a.m. tomorrow with inst. They will meet Batt. at Road Junction M.3.c.2.3. at 10.30 a.m. 15th inst.

3. Battalion will move by Coys. at 100 yards interval on 15th inst. in order A.B.C.D. Coys. Transport will follow 100 yards in rear of D. Coy. A Coy. will not close up to less than 500 yards from Transport of 3rd Queens.
   Signallers & Runners will march in rear of A. Coy. Drums in front of B. Coy. Pioneers in rear of D Coy. Remainder of H.Q. in rear of B. Coy.
   'A' Coy will start from Junction of tracks to farms and HALLEBAST - OUDERDOM road by 8.55 a.m. & will pass road junction H.32.d.8.1. at 9.15 a.m.
   Dress:- Full Marching Order.

4. Rations will be carried on the Cookers.

5. 2 Lorries will report at MICMAC CAMP at 8 a.m. 15th inst. for Stores.
   Blankets in bundles of 10 will be at Q.M. Stores at 8 a.m.
   Coy. Stores & Officers Valises at same time & place.
   Mess Baskets will be collected at 8.15 a.m.
   Orderly Room Stores & R.A.P. Stores will be collected at 8.15 a.m.

6. O.C. B. Coy. will detail a loading party of 1 N.C.O. & 20 men to be at Q.M. Stores by 8 a.m. 15th inst.

7. The strictest march discipline must be maintained. First halt will be at 9.50 a.m. & afterwards 10 minutes to each hour.

(Signed) H. Bass
Captain & Adjt.
10th York R.

10th Yorkshire Regt.

Addition to Order 84.   15.10.17

1. Two lorries will be at disposal of Battn. [...]
Quarter Master will arrange for [...] same at Bde. H.Q 2
at 7 am
   Officers kits & Men's kits will be at Q.M. Stores by 7 am
   O.C. "C" Coy will detail a loading party [...] N.C.O and
12 men who will report at Q.M. Stores by 7 am
   If lorries are late a guard will be detailed by R.S.M
from "C" Coys loading party

2. Battalion will continue the march on the 16 [...]
   bivouac and [...] 11th to the BARLIN [...]

Distribution
1, 2 & 3 [...]
4, 5, 6, 7 Coys
8 [...]
9 & [...]
10 M.O
11 Sig. Off
12 Asst. Adj (for information)

[signed]
[...] Battn. 10th Yorks R.

SECRET.   10th Yorkshire Regt   4   Copy No.

Marker Haisebrouck 60 tooo   Order No 84
       Sheet 28. 1/40,000   13.11.17

1.   21st Division will move from 2nd Army to 1st Army Area on the 14th inst, and on arrival will join the XIII Corps.
2.   10th York R will move to new billets on that date.
3.   Battalion will move by Coys. at 100 yards interval in order A. C. D. B. Transport passing starting point, road junction 9C Central at 8.31 am.
     Signals & Runners will march in front of B. Drums in front of D. Pioneers behind A. Other H.Q. details behind C.
     B Coy will leave camp at 8.15 am.
4.   Route via WESTOUTRE - LOCRE - BAILLEUL & OUTERSTEEN.
5.   Batt. will halt at 10 minutes before each hour and will resume march at the clock hour.
6.   Guides will meet the Batt. at Cross Roads south of O. in OUTERSTEEN.
7.   Officers valises will be loaded by 7.15 am. Blankets at 7.15 am. Mess Carts will be collected at 7.45 a.m.
8.   Orders re billeting parties and guides will be notified later.

Distribution
1.2.3 War Diary & File
4.5.6.7. Coys
8. QM
9. T.O
10 M.O
11 Spec. Off
12. 62 Inf. Bde (for information)

                              Captain & Adjutant
                              10th York R.

SECRET   J   Sep   3

Ref.   10th Yorkshire Regt. Order No. 85

5A

I   10 York R will march, route march to RUSAO's ROOST
    tomorrow 18th inst.
        Order of March C D A Coys detachments as per
    today. Dress – marching order less packs.
    Starting Point X road. 1/2 mile west of ……
    first Coy will pass starting point at 9.45 a.m. Rendezvous
    will be maintained between Coys. Transport …
    When transport marches separately, 100 yds.
    between transport & latter will be maintained.

2. A billeting party consisting of 1A CO per Coy + HQ
    under Lt. C. Pepper accompanied by RSM … will
    proceed by lorry leaving Bde HQ at 10 … a.m tomorrow

3. Three lorries have been allotted to the Bn – guides for same
    to be at Bde HQ at 8 a.m. These lorries will make
    double journeys.

4. All blankets, greatcoats, and surplus packs of Coys will
    be dumped at ……… to be carried at 6 a.m.
    tomorrow. Stores of HQ will be outside Adjs billet at
    the same time. One … will be detailed to
    guard same …. be picked up by lorry.
    These baggages will be collected at 9 a.m.

5. Rations will be carried on cookers

6. Strict march discipline will be maintained

                                    A Ham Capt & Adj
    Distribution
    Copy No 1 + 2 Wardens & file   10 York R
         "   3 O C Coys
         "   8   150
         "   9   440
         "   10   TD
         "   11   G..
         "   12   TD
         "   13   …
         "   14   …   H & file

SECRET.   10th Bn. Yorkshire Regt   K   Copy No. 2

Map Ref. { HAZEBROUCK 5A
           LENS 11.   Order No 86.   18.11.17.

1. Battalion will move by Route March to BARLIN area on the 19th inst.

2. Order of march. D.A.B.C Coys & Transports. Detachments as for today.
   Dress will be notified later.

3. Battalion will form up with head of column, at Cross roads, ¼ mile due South of I in VENDIN-LES-B. YUNE ready to march off at 8.30 a.m. facing S.E.

4. Officers Kits and Blankets to be at Q.M. Stores by 7.30 a.m. Mess Baskets will be collected at 8 a.m.

5. Orders regarding billeting party will be notified later. 1 N.C.O & per Coy & N.B. under 2 Lieut Hart to be held in readiness.

6. It was noticed today that all Officers' servants were very late, several joining Battn. after march had begun. Mess Presidents must arrange breakfasts at such a time, that all Mess baskets are ready to be collected at time arranged.

Distribution
1.2.3 War Diary & File
4.5.6.7 Coys.
8. M.O
9. T.O
10. 2.M.
11. Spec. Offrs.
12. (62 Inf Bde (for information)

Captain & Adjutant
10th York.R.

SECRET.   10th Bn. Yorkshire Regt   K   Copy No 3

                        Addition to Order 86   18.11.17

1. Billeting party, as detailed will be at ANNEZIN CHURCH
at 7.30 am. where they will be picked up by lorries, and
taken to billets in HERSIN.

2. Packs will be dumped at same time and place as
Officers kits.

3. Route:- via ANNEZIN — VAUDRICOURT — HOUCHIN —
BARLIN — BILLETS HERSIN. (COUPIGNY HUTS).

4. Lorries. It is hoped to secure lorries as for today.
if guides are required details will be & later. (See No 6).

5. Billeting party will meet Batt. at entrance to HERSIN on BARLIN-
HERSIN ROAD.

6. Quarter Master will arrange for guides for lorries to be at
GONNEHEM CHURCH at 8.0 am. Lorries will do two journeys.

7. Ration wagons will be picked up by Transport Officer
at Cross Roads South of T in HALLICOURT.
Transport route via HAILLICOURT.

Distribution
1. 2. 3 War Diary & file
4. 5. 6. 7 Companies
8   MO
9   TO
10 QM
11 Lewis O.
12 62 Inf Bde (for Info).

                                    H. Bass Captain & Adjutant
                                              10th York R.

Copy No 1

I SECRET

10th YORKSHIRE REGT
Order No 87
19.11.17

MAP REF
LENS. 11

1. 62 Infty Bde will move by route march to huts in Mt ST ELOY AREA tomorrow in the order 12/13 NORTH. FUS. 10th YORK R. 1 LINC'S Rgt. etc

2. 10th York R. will pass Bde starting point X roads VERDREL FORAGE one mile south of COUPIGNY CHATEAU at 10.38. Order of march A.B.C.D. Coys, detachments as usual. First Coy will leave Camp just in rear of 12/13 NORTH. FUS. at 10.15.
Dress marching order less packs

3. Transport will be Brigaded under Bde Transport Officer & will march in order of Battns, passing the above starting point at 9.30 AM. Ration wagons will be picked up at railway crossing 1 mile N.W. of VILLERS au Bois

4. Billeting party 1 N.C.O per Coy + N.C.O H.Q. (to be detailed by Lt E. Pepper) under Lt Pepper will meet Staff Capt 62nd Bde at Area Commandant's Office at Mt ST ELOY. Cycles will be taken.
A further billeting party under 2nd Lt Hart will be ready to move off tomorrow afternoon to take over huts from 142 Bde at ECURIE. Further orders will be issued later

5. Three lorries to do double journeys will report at entrance to COUPIGNY HUTS CAMP at 8.15.
Blankets & mess kits will be dumped there at 8.15.
T.O. will arrange to collect valises of Officers billeted in the Town & Mess Baskets by 8.15.

Distribution
Copy 1 2 3   War Diary File
     4 5 6 7 O.C. Coys
     8   2 i/c
     9   T.O.
     10   S.O.
     11   R.O.
     12   L & O
     13   M.O.
     14   62nd Infty Bde

H Bass
Capt & Adjt
10th York R

Copy No. 2   10 YORKSHIRE REGT.   SECRET
                                                                              20.11.17
MAP REF.   Order 88   M
51 B 51 C

I   10th York R will move by route march to WAKEFIELD CAMP
        A 28 c 5.8 tomorrow 21st inst.
        Order of march B C D A Coys detachments as for today
        Batt. will be formed up facing S.E. with head of column
        at road junction F 8.c 87 ready to move off at 9.20 a.m.
        Dress   Marching order less packs.

                                                          church
II   Two lorries to do double journeys will report at Mt St Eloy
        at 8 a.m.   2 M. will detail guide for same
        Officers Kits Blankets & mens packs will be dumped at 2 M
        Stores by 8 a.m.

III   Mess Baskets will be collected at 9 a.m.

IV   Lewis Gun Officer will arrange to relieve two Lewis
        Gun anti aircraft Gun detachments (that is two Guns)
        at A 29 c 52 as soon as possible after arrival in
        Camp. he will report relief complete to H Q.

                                              H Baw
                                              Capt - Adjt -
Distribution
                                              10 York R
Copy   1. 2. 3   War Diary File
        4 5 6 7   O C Coys
        8   S O
        9   T O
        10   2 M
        11   M O
        12   62 Infy Bde

SECRET   10th Yorkshire Regt.   N°   Copy ....
FOOT 9/100
MAP REF Sheet 20,000   Order A 2   23·11·17

1. (a) If the operations now in progress on the 3rd Army front attain further
success, it is possible that the enemy may withdraw opposite 13th Corps front.
   If such a withdrawal takes place the most probable lines on
which it would be carried out appears to be as follows:-
(1) Pivoting on FRESNOY along the general line of the FRESNES-
ROUVROY line, with a possibility of a further retirement to a new
switch line which has been dug from C 21 b through C 22, C 23 and
C 24 to connect with the DROCOURT - QUEANT line.
(2) A withdrawal following on (1) to the DROCOURT - QUEANT line.
(b) The 31st Div. now holding the 13th Corps front, has been ordered to be ready.
If the enemy retires to advance as follows:-
   1st Objective   YELLOW LINE ON MAP.
   2nd   "   GREEN   "
In the event of the 31st Div. moving forward the 21st Div. will co-operate.
62nd Bde on Right 64th Bde on Left. 110th Bde in Reserve. Boundaries
between Bdes & Batts are shown on attached maps.

2. The task of the 62 Bde, in conjunction with 64 Bde will be either:-
(a) To support the advance of the 31st Div.
(b) If required to push forward through the 31 Div & carry on the advance or
(c) Be prepared to hold our present trench system in case of necessity.

3. On receipt of orders to move 10 York R. will move to positions of assembly
as follows.
   EARL TRENCH   A Coy Right D Coy Left.
   VISCOUNT St.   C   "   B   "
      "   "   1 sect. 62 M.G.C.
      "   "   Batt H.Q. (present H Q 11 E Lancs).
12/13 North'd Fus. will be on the Right of the Batt. in MARINE TRENCH
& the 64 Bde on the left.
   From these positions the Batt. will be in readiness to carry out
either of those missions assigned to it.

4. The 11th E. Lancs are now holding the line as under:-
1 Coy.   Bradford Post.   2 Sections   Bird Post.   1 Coy Beatty Post.
1 Coy (less 2 Sec) Earl Trench
Close liaison will be maintained by small patrols, both with units
on the flank & to units in front as under.
A Coy. - With a Coy of E Lancs in Bradford Post & Bird Post
D "   -   Beatty Post
C "   -   12/13 North'd Fus.
B "   -   batt of 64 Bde on our immediate left

(2)

5. Instructions regarding reconnaissance have already been issued.

6. In the event of the 62 Bde. taking over the present trench system from the 92 & 93 Bde (para 2(c)), the 10th York R. will take over from the 11 E. Lancs as under:-

   A Coy.   Bradford Post
   1 Plat /C.   Bird Post.
   D Coy.   Beatty Post.
   B Coy.   Earl Trench
   C Coy (less 1 Plat)   Earl Trench
   Bn. H.Q.   Viscount St.

7. A Reg. Aid Post will be established near the existing Aid Post of the 11° E Lancs.

8. The Batt. Signal Officer will make the necessary arrangements for Communication paying particular attention to visual signalling possibilities.

9. 62 Inf Bde H.Q. will on receipt of orders to move forward be established at MAISON BLANCHE.

Distribution
1, 2, 3   War Diary & file
4, 5, 6, 7   Coy.
8.   M.O.
9.   T.O.
10. 2 m.
11. I.O.
12   62 Inf Bde (for Information).

H Dass
Captain & Adjt
10 York R.

Copy *[illegible]*   10th Yorkshire Regt.   Sheet 57

After 27/8/MD   Naulin 2 Oct 92   [illegible]

1. The following part of instructions is issued.

ROUTE
The question of the route to be followed will depend on the action of the enemy artillery, whether the move is by day or night.

(a) The following route is under cover the whole way.
Cross Roads at B.28.a.6. & POZIERES—COURCELETTE road B.23.c.9. along the road *[illegible]* BUTTE ROAD up to B.14.9 — leave the road and move due East into the Railway cutting, just North of B.15.30 in MAISON BLANCHE. March along the cutting Northwards, up to station at B.28.c.8.8. then along the trench and sunk road track, which follows the Railway *[illegible]* or to Western side up to B.16.c.7.8. under the railway by the kennel, into OUSE ALLEY, and thence by the communication trench to the front line.

(b) It is understood that there is a newly made road, running from COURCELETTE through squares B.20.a.b, B.19.c, B.19.b, B.20.a. where meets OUSE ALLEY.

(c) Any other course *[illegible]* advance over the open in Artillery formation. COPSE WOOD is a good landmark.
One Officer per Coy will reconnoitre, and to all roads, as far as the Western end of OUSE ALLEY, tomorrow morning. Short reports on the results of reconnaissances will be forwarded to Orderly Room on completion.

Ration and stores will be located on to the Light Railway at CHANTICLERS GATE. Transport Officer will reconnoitre this point tomorrow.

Copy of [illegible] words
for following:

From this point they will be carried up to a point in the Rockies about 500 yards S. of OUSE ALLEY. From the Mule Carriers will push the Rations up *[illegible]* to *[illegible]* a point 100 yds from Batt. HQ in VISCOUNT ST.

3. Water is to dump to a point in OUSE ALLEY 400 yds N. of the junction of OUSE ALLEY & VISCOUNT ST.

4. The Batt. Aid Post is in VISCOUNT ST at B.16.c.2.7.

5. The Battn. S.A.A. & Grenade dumps is in NORTH TYNE TRENCH about 100 yds from its junction with VISCOUNT ST.

[signature]
Capt. & Adjt
4th Yorks Regt.

SECRET
Copy No. 3:   30.11.17
MAP REF   10th York Regt Orders No 2
LENS 11
VALENCIENNES
_____

1   62 Infty Bde will move by train today to
        BEAUMENCOURT

2   The following transport will accompany units on the train
     3 Cookers 2 L.G.S. wagons for S.A.A. 1 Medical cart
     2 Chargers 2 pack animals
     This transport will be at entraining station at Marceuil
     by 11 pm & leave at 2 am Dec 1st.

3   All other first line transport will draw rations by
     7 pm.

4   10th York R. will move by train leaving Marceuil
     at 3 am Dec 1st, and will be at Station by 2 am
     Bn will be formed up with head of column at WATER
     POINT at H.2. ready to move off at ½ midnight
     Order of March   A. B. C. D. Coys H. Q. & details
     Coy Comds will render in entraining state to H.2 by
     8 pm tonight

5   Advance Party consisting of 1 N.C.O. per Coy & one for
     H.2 under 2nd Lt R. A. James, will leave H.2 at
     11 pm. eyelets will be taken.

6   Lewis Guns will be taken by hand

7   Rations for tomorrow will be carried on the man

8   All Blankets & surplus stores will be packed in the hut
     in D Coy's line. O.C. B Coy will detail two
     men to report to Sergt Barton at the Canteen & these
     will be left in charge of stores.
          Lorries for blankets etc will probably be available

Distribution
Copy 1, 2, 3 War Diary. File
  " 4, 5, 6, 7 OC Coys
  " 8   2 i/c
                                            Harris Copeman
                                            Lt Col
                                            10 York R.

Army Form C. 2118.

WAR DIARY
or
INTELLIGENCE SUMMARY.
(*Erase heading not required.*)

10 Bn Yorkshire Regt
for month of
Dec. 1917

67.B.
13 sheets

Army Form C. 2118.

WAR DIARY
or
INTELLIGENCE SUMMARY.
(Erase heading not required.)

Instructions regarding War Diaries and Intelligence Summaries are contained in F. S. Regs., Part II. and the Staff Manual respectively. Title pages will be prepared in manuscript.

Place	Date	Hour	Summary of Events and Information	Remarks and references to Appendices
BRUSLE	1.12.17		Bn. arrived PERONNE at 12.30pm and detrained. Lt. for. marched after an hours halt to BRUSLE (5 miles) where it went into huts.	
"	2.12.17		Bn. ans not more. Day was spent in cleaning up etc.	
"	3.12.17		Bn. moved at 2pm to LONGAVESNES. Co. proceeded to reconnoitre defences for turns in Case of necessity between EPEHY and HEUDICOURT	1
LONGAVESNES	4.12.17		Co. and Coy. Comdr. reconnoitred line to be taken up when in bn. Reserve in Case of enemy attack. Bn. rested.	
"	5.12.17		Bn. carried out training.	
"	6.12.17		Bn. moved to HEUDICOURT. Co. reconnoitred defensive line at HILL 140.	2
"	7.12.17		Orders recd. to relieve 9th R.O.Y.L.I. in line E. of PEZIERES night 9/10 Dec. Co.	

Army Form C. 2118.

WAR DIARY
or
INTELLIGENCE SUMMARY.
(Erase heading not required.)

Place	Date	Hour	Summary of Events and Information	Remarks and references to Appendices
MEDDICOURT	7.12.17		Reconnoitred his line by O.C. "Y" Co.	
"	8.12.17		O.C. and Co. Comdrs. went and took over line held by O.C.s "Y" & "L" and completed arrangements for relief.	
"	9.12.17		Bn. relieved 9 Roy L.I. Co. detailed in Order No. 5. Complete by 6.30pm. Quiet night except for some shelling of ENEMY in which 5 of our "Gunners" were wounded.	3
"	10.12.17		Very quiet day. Enemy sniping and artillery very inactive. Our patrols active at night but report that no enemy.	
"	11.12.17		Quiet. At night men saw some shelling of works to our Very cold. Quiet day. Oct 1913 Ambulances From and Co. Comdrs. Reconnoitred line, and made arrangements for relief next 18.12 Dec.	
"	12.12.17		At night an escaped prisoner of war (with the French) was captured by No. 29265 Cpl. BUCKLEY ("B" Co.) near our front line.	

WAR DIARY
or
INTELLIGENCE SUMMARY.
(Erase heading not required.)

Army Form C. 2118.

Place	Date	Hour	Summary of Events and Information	Remarks and references to Appendices
Trenches	13.12.17		About 6 am. No. 23515A Sgt. T.W. THOMPSON and No. 242635 Cpl. B. BUCKLEY (both of "B" Coy) unearthed a German post 400 yds from our line E. of VILLERS-GUISLAINS and brought back a report that it is twenty one posts, and that the men that approach our relief. 2Lt. T.D. SMITH immediately called for volunteers for a Raiding Party, and he, 2 N.C.O.'s mentioned above and 3 9/10s. (No. 23447 Pte. T. KING, No. 36134 Pte. H. TURNER, No. 36110 Pte. N. BACON) all went out to the party consisting of 6 all told then went out in broad daylight, penetrated the German and after a personal reconnaissance by 2Lt. SMITH attacked the German post. 13 Germans were killed and one brought back to our line unwounded. Pte. 17913 N. Pte. reconnoitred him in morning. Being by 17913 N. Pte. complete at 5.50 p.m. Br. Or. Wolff was disabled as fireman. "D" Coy CAVALRY LINE "A" Coy. BROWN LINE, H.Q. and A-A Coy. Ry. Embankment. (Sh. 23. 6)	+
"	14.12.17		Co. + Co. Comdr. Reconnection were held by 3/4 the Queen's R. (MICHELETTE F") and made arrangements for relief night 15/16	

2353 Wt. W2344/1454 700,000 5/15 D.D.&L. A.D.S.S./Forms/C. 2118.

WAR DIARY
or
INTELLIGENCE SUMMARY.
(Erase heading not required.)

Army Form C. 2118.

Place	Date	Hour	Summary of Events and Information	Remarks and references to Appendices
Rly. Embankment (A.23.d)	15.12.17		Relief of 8/4 The Queens Regt complete at 7p.m. Very cold. Quiet night.	5
"	16.12.17		Enemy very inactive. At night the artillery of the Corps carried out a shoot on VILLERS GUISLAIN. No prisoners have reported a relief. O.C. 10 K.O.Y.LI. and O.C. Comdrs. reconnoitred line. Bn H.Q. of 3 S.R. at grown Pm.	
"	17.12.17		Relief by 10 K.O.Y.LI. complete at 7p.m. Enemy shelled the approaches during the relief. Lieut. SARSON being wounded. Being early morning a shell obtained a direct hit on the orderly room. Our casualties for day. Or: on R.Sher Lt Sarson, +3 O.R. wounded. O.R. relief Bn. proceeded to camp in LONGAVESNES. Very cold night. Snow + sleet.	6
LONGAVESNES	18.12.17		Bn rested and cleaned up.	
"	19.12.17		Hard frost and very cold. Bn. rested. C.O. Mr. Lt. Colonel R. CUMMING proceeded to England on posting to home establishment. 2/Lt. A.E.S. CLIFTON acting C.O. Mr.	
"	20.12.17		Carried out a short route march.	

Army Form C. 2118.

WAR DIARY
or
INTELLIGENCE SUMMARY.
(Erase heading not required.)

Instructions regarding War Diaries and Intelligence Summaries are contained in F. S. Regs., Part II. and the Staff Manual respectively. Title pages will be prepared in manuscript.

Place	Date	Hour	Summary of Events and Information	Remarks and references to Appendices
LONDON Rs Nr 21.12.17			Bn. arrived out camp	
"	22.12.17.		Bn. moved to LIERMONT and housed in huts	
"	23.12.17.		All Coys. dug shelter and sandbagged huts. Special instruction given to Lewis Gr. R.E. Lt SMIESMITH and STOCKHAM on Strength of Bn. from 2.12.17.	
"	24.12.17		Strength of SLt. and instruction to Lewis continued	
"	25.12.17.		Xmas day. Divine service in hangar. Information recd. that No 30740 Pte H. TURNER, No 29247 A/G. T. RICE and No 36452 L/Cpl HOSKINS had been awarded the Military Medal for their share in the raid carried out on the morning of the 18th Dec.	
"	26.12.17.		The Bn. wheeled 15 Bn. J. M. Rifles Snb section. Relief complete at 6.30 p. Quiet night	7
"	27.12.17.		Fog cold. Quiet day. Enemy inactive	
"	28.12.17.		Bitterly cold. Some enemy artillery acting on enemy. Bn. H.Q. and Coys.	

WAR DIARY
or
INTELLIGENCE SUMMARY.
(Erase heading not required.)

Army Form C. 2118.

Place	Date	Hour	Summary of Events and Information	Remarks and references to Appendices
Trenches	29.12.17		Coy. Comdr. 1st Lincolnshire Regt. reconnoitred line to be relieved by 1 Lincolnshire Regt. Completed at 6 p.m. Pr on W/cof Districts as follows: C. Co. BROWN LINE, H.Q. + A.B + D coys Reg Embankment (k.236)	
"	30.12.17		Co. + Coy Comdrs reconnoitred BROWN and QUARRY LINES. Very Quiet.	
"	31.12.17		Co. reconnoitred left Subsection (BIRCH AVE + COPSE to CHAPEL ST) held by coys in Res. King's Pals of 111 O.T.R formed to 103 Thundery Coy still in Bn. Reserve.	

R. Murray (?)
O. in C. 9th (?)

Copy No...3.
Map 62c

10th YORKSHIRE REGIMENT ORDER No 3.   SECRET.
3.12.17

1. 10th York R will move to camp in LONGAVESNES today.

2. Bn. will be formed up on road ready to move off at 1.15p.m. Order of march "B" "C" "D" "A" Coys H.Q. Details & Transport. Dress - Full marching Order Great Coats will be worn.

3. Mess baskets will be collected at 12.45p.m.

4. Route - X roads BOUCLY - X roads TINCOURT LONGAVESNES.

(Sgd) H.Bass Capt & Adj
10th York R.

Distribution
Copy Nos 1.2.3. War diary & File
    3.4.5.6. O C.Coys
       7 Spec Offrs
       8 Q.M
       9 T.O
     10 I.o
     11 62 Bde (for information)

SECRET.   10 Yorkshire Regt. Order No 4   Copy No.

Map Ref: Sheet
57c v 62c 1/40.000   6th December 1917

1. 1st Lincoln Regt & 10th York Regt will move to HEUDECOURT by route march to-day.

2. Batt will move by Companies at 300 yards interval, first Company to pass starting point. Cross Roads E 19 a 9.1 at 2.45 pm Order of march C D A B Coys. details from post.

3. 4 G.S. Wagons will report at 2 pm for blankets.

4. All Officers kits and blankets rolled in bundles of 10 will be at Q.M. Stores at 1 pm.
    Men Baskets will be collected at 2.15 pm.

5. Route: LONGAVESNES — LIERAMONT — HEUDECOURT.

6. Bivouacs and tents will be thoroughly cleaned & left standing. O.C. 'B' Coy will detail guard of 1 NCO & 3 men to guard same. They will be rationed for 24 hrs.

7. Rations will be carried on Cookers & not on the men.

8. Stores that cannot be taken will be stacked together, one man from Q.M. Stores will be left in charge.

9. Dress. Full marching order. Great coats will not be worn.

                        Signed
                        H Barr. Captain & Adjt
                        10 York R.

Correction to Order No 4.

1. For starting point read:- E 25 b 13. First Coy will pass starting point at 2.30 pm.

2. Men baskets will be collected at 2 pm.

                        Signed
                        H Barr Captn & Adjt
                        10 York R.

SECRET   10th Yorkshire Regt   Copy No. 1.
Map Ref. Sheet   Order No 5.   8.12.17
57c S.E 1/10000

1. 10th York R will relieve the 9th K.O.Y.L.I. on the night of the 9/10th December 1917 in the right sub-section.
   'A' Coy 10th York R will relieve C Coy on the right
   'B'   "   "   "   "   B "   in the centre
   'D'   "   "   "   "   A "   on the left.
   'C'   "   "   "   "   D "   in support trenches.
   Order of relief, left sector, right sector, centre sector, support & Batt. H.Q.
   A.B & C Coys Cookers will leave present billets at 12 p.m.
   Signal will leave present billets at 2.15 p.m. so as to complete relief by daylight.

2. Guides. 2 per Coy. 1 for H.Q. will be at H.Q. 62nd Infty Bde. HEUDECOURT at 4.30 p.m. on 9th inst. Arrangements will be made for these guides to be at Bn H.Q. at 4.35 p.m. 'D' Coy will move off at that time.

3. Water Cart will be kept full at Bn H.Q. (also a reserve in petrol tins) it will refill at the Square HEUDECOURT.

4. Rations will be delivered at Transport Lines and taken up to Bn H.Q. W30 a 0.2 by First Line Transport. Rations for the 10th will be carried on Cookers.

5. Transport will take over from the 10th K.O.Y.L.I. at VILLERS-FAUCON on the 9th inst. Relief will be complete by 12 noon.

6. 'D' Coy will have dinner & cook in railway cutting X 19 a 25.60.

7. Blankets & officers kits will be dumped at I.M Stores by 10 a.m

8. Mess Baskets   do   do   do
   Trench kits & mess baskets for trenches will be collected at 12 p.m.

9. 20 Magazines per Lewis Gun will be taken over on relief.
   1 L.G. N.C.O. will remain at present billets to hand over same number to the 9th K.O.Y.L.I. unless taken over before Bn. moves off. Receipts will be taken for these.

10. 62nd Infantry Bde. R.E. dump will be W17 c 3.2. 21st Div. dump ROISEL.
    S.A.A & bomb dumps:- W 16 c 9.1 W 17 c 9.2.
    There is also a dump at W 18 d 2.2. which can only be drawn on in case of emergency.

11. Burial ground X 19 a 3.8.

12. 1 Officer, 2 N.C.Os per Coy. will report to Bn H.Q. 9th K.O.Y.L.I. at 11 a.m on the 9th inst and will remain in the line.

13. All grenades, rifle grenades, S.A.A. S.O.S. Signs. Maps, defence schemes etc. will be taken over on relief.

14. O.C. 'D' Coy will arrange to leave a guard of 1 N.C.O & 3. O.R. at Bn R.E dump X 13 c 3.1

15. Dress. Battle Order, Great Coats, jerkins will be rolled with waterproof sheets and strapped on the belt at back.

16. Dry socks will be issued each morning & O.C. Coys must see that wet ones are ready to be returned for drying.

17. Transport Off. of 9th K.O.Y.L.I. will draw from 10th YORK R. 80 buckets L.G. Magazines & 40 petrol tins, sometime tomorrow 9th inst. Receipts will be obtained for these.

                         R.A. James 2/Lieut. Asst Adjt
                                  10 York. R.

SECRET.   10th YORKSHIRE REGIMENT.   Copy No.......

Map Ref. Sheet   ORDER No. 8
57c S.E.1/20000.

1.   10th York R. will be relieved by 10th K.O.Y.L.I. on the night of the 17/18th December 1917.
        Coys. will be relieved as follows and in the following order:-
'C' Coy. 10th York R. (L. Front Sector) will be relieved by 'D' Coy. 10th K.O.Y.L.I.
'A' Coy. 10th York R. (Right Front Sector) will be relieved by 'B' Coy. 10th K.O.Y.L.I.
'B' Coy. 10th York R. R. Support will be relieved by 'A' Coy. 10th K.O.Y.L.I.
'D' Coy. 10th York R. L. Support will be relieved by 'C' Coy. 10th K.O.Y.L.I.
        Relief complete will be notified by code word "CHEERS"

2.   Upon relief Bn. moves to camp at LONGAVESNES.
        Coys. will move there via road running through W.22. W.28. & E.4. (if wet via HEUDECOURT & SAULCOURT)

3.   Guides. 1 per platoon from 'A''C' & 'B' Coys. will meet relieving Coys. of 10th K.O.Y.L.I. at X Roads near Bn. H.Q. at 5.30 p.m
        Advance parties from 10th K.O.Y.L.I. will report at Bn. H.Q. on 17th at 2.30 p.m. and guides will take them to their respective sectors.
        Advance parties of 10th York R. consisting of 1 officer, 1 N.C.O. per Coy. and H.Q. will report to H.Q. 10th K.O.Y.L.I. at LONGAVESNES. to take over the camp, they will meet Coys. coming into camp.
        Coy. Q.M. Sgts. will also report there as early as possible.

4.   Dinners on 17th at 12 noon, tea 3.30 p.m.
        Transport Officer will make following arrangements:-
Coy. Officers chargers will be at RAILTON X Roads at 6 p.m.
C.O. Adjt. & M.O.   "   "   "   at 7 p.m.
        All officers trench kits will be at Bn. H.Q. by 2 p.m. Limbers will collect these and H.Q. mess baskets at 2.30 p.m.
        Coy. mess baskets, cooking utensils, Bn. petrol tins etc. will be dumped at Bn. H.Q. by 4.15 p.m. and collected by limber at 4.30 p.m.
        Lewis Gun limbers will be on road 300 yards W. of X roads W.18.d.8.1. at 5.30 p.m.
        10th K.O.Y.L.I. will relieve guard 2 N.C.Os. and 3 men on Bde. R.E. dump at W.18.d.8.1.
        All grenades, S.A.A., S.O.S. Signals. tools. defence schemes, maps showing defences will be handed over.
        Report of work done during tour, and work programme will be handed over, copy will be sent to Bn. H.Q. by 2 p.m. December 17th.

                                            2/Lieut. Actg Adjt.
16.12.17.   10th YORK R.

Distribution:-
    1,2 & 3 War Diary & File.
    4,5,6,7 O.C. Coys.
      8.   T.O.
      9.   M.O.
     10   Q.M.
     11   Specialists.
     12 62nd Infantry Brigade (for information)

SECRET

MAP REF.
57c. S.E. 1/10000

10th Yorkshire Regiment
Order No. 10.

Copy No.

1. 10th YORK R. will relieve 15th DURHAM LIGHT INFANTRY on the night of 26/27th Dec. 1917 in the right sub sector.
   Coys. will relieve as follows & in the following order:-
   'B' Coy. 10th YORK R. (RIGHT FRONT) will relieve 'C' Coy. 15th D.L.I.
   'D'   (LEFT FRONT)   'B'
   'C'   (LEFT SUPPORT)   'D'
   'A'   (RES. SUPPORT)   'A'
   Relief complete will be notified by the word 'YEAR'.

2. Guides for 'B' & 'A' Coys. will be at Coys' mess W.23.b.4.1.
   Lewis Gun limbers will dump guns for these Coys at same place.
   Guides for 'D' & 'C' Coys will be picked up at RAILTON X ROADS at 4-30.
   L.G. limbers will dump guns 300 yards W. of X roads W.h.15.c.1.
   Advance parties from 10 YORK R. 1 officer 2 o.r. per coy. + H.Q. will report to 15th D.L.I. Bn. H.Q. at noon on 26th. These parties will take over all grenades. S.A.A. S.O.S. Signals, lists, defence schemes, codes, maps showing dispositions by day & night.
   Advance parties from 15th D.L.I. will report to 10th YORK R. Bn H.Q. to take over same at 12 noon on 26th.

3. Signals will leave camp at 2-15 so as to complete the relief by daylight.
   Coys. will move at 5 minutes interval 'B' Coy leaving camp at 2.45 to pass RAILTON X ROADS at 4-30 from that point Bn will move by platoons at 100 yards interval.
   Dinners at 1 p.m. Tea will be had in trenches.
   Cookers will move directly after dinner.
   All men will rub their feet with whale oil before going into the line.

4. Dress: Batt. Order. Great coats will be worn & jerkins carried.

5. 100 petrol tins will be taken over in the line & 100 handed over in exchange in camp.
   D. & C. Coys will cook in support at X.19.a.3.8.
   A. & B. Coys cookers will stand at RAILWAY EMBANKMENT W.23.b.4.1.
   H.Q. will cook in dixies at Bn. H.Q.
   Transport Officer will arrange transport for D.C. & H.Q. dixies.
   Trench Kits & Trench Mess Baskets will be dumped at Bn HQ at 2 p.m.
   Blankets folded tightly in bundles of 10 & mens packs will be dumped at Q.M. stores by 10 a.m.
   Water cart will be kept full at the cookers & will refill at HEUDECOURT.

6. Camp will be left scrupulously clean. Certificate to that effect will be obtained from incoming unit.

R.C. James 2/Lieut. Actg. Adjt.
10 York R.

WAR DIARY
or
INTELLIGENCE SUMMARY.

(Erase heading not required.)

Army Form C. 2118.

Place	Date	Hour	Summary of Events and Information	Remarks and references to Appendices
FIELD	JANUARY 1916			
	1st	—	Bn. in Brigade Support on Railway Embankment at W.23.E.	M&B 57.c S24
	2nd	—	Relieved. 12/13 Bn. NORTHUMBERLAND FUSILIERS. Bn. left west over (see plan)	O.O. 1028 attached
	3rd 5th 7th	—	Hostile artillery active. Very cold. Fairly quiet period. Very foggy later. Much aerial activity on 3rd.	
	8th	—	Bn. relieved by 12/13 Bn. N. Fus. + moved back to emergency Quiet period in camp. Bn. billets + church up.	M.S. 57c. 5.24 O.O. H2 14
	9th 10th 11th	—	at HEUDECOURT.	
	12th	—	Bn. relieved 12/13 Bn. N. Fus. in left subsection (front line from X.7.c.30.90. to X.13.b.40.10. support line from X.13.a.20.70 to X.13.b.	O.O. Nº 55 attached. M.S 57c. S.E.4
	13th 14th 15th	—	Support Company in trenches in W.19.B. Reserve Coy in trenches	
	16th	—	Bn. relieved by 12/13 Bn. N. Fus. + moved (two Coys B & C) to BEZIERS to Railway Embankment in W.23.E.	O.O. Nº 55.a attached M.S. 57c. SE.4.

28B
17 sheet

Army Form C. 2118.

WAR DIARY
or
INTELLIGENCE SUMMARY.
(Erase heading not required.)

Instructions regarding War Diaries and Intelligence Summaries are contained in F.S. Regs., Part II. and the Staff Manual respectively. Title pages will be prepared in manuscript.

Place	Date	Hour	Summary of Events and Information	Remarks and references to Appendices
FIELD			**JAN 1916**	
	17th to 19th	—	Quiet period. Working parties found for R.E.	O.O. N° 216 attached
	20th	—	Bn. relieved 12/13th Bn. Y. Fus. in Leipzig Redoubt	
	21st to 23rd	—	Quiet period. Much aerial activity on 22nd.	
	24th	—	Bn. relieved by 13/18th Bn. N. Fus. & moved back to & occupied HEODECOURT & Thurcoing Brigade Reserve. Quiet Period.	J. Diaries attached. N° 270 & 4.
	25th to 27th	—	Bn. relieved 12/13th N. Fus. in Leipzig Redoubt. Comp. Combat just before relieving. Two Entanglements during relief. No casualties.	O.O. N° 29
	28th	—	Quiet day.	
	29th 30th	—	Bn. relieved by 16th Bn. RIFLE BRIGADE & proceed Bus to MOISLAINS & at HECOURT for (illegible).	O.O. N° 2-45 M. & 57 & 58 & AMIEN 22
	31st	—	Bn. cleaning up.	

Army Form C. 2118.

WAR DIARY
or
INTELLIGENCE SUMMARY.
(Erase heading not required.)

Instructions regarding War Diaries and Intelligence Summaries are contained in F. S. Regs., Part II. and the Staff Manual respectively. Title pages will be prepared in manuscript.

N° 3

Place	Date	Hour	Summary of Events and Information	Remarks and references to Appendices
FIELD			ADMINISTRATIVE	
	5th		Draft of 85 O.R. arrived & posted to Coys. (29/12/17) (cancelled) 2nd Lt. A. WRAY. Killed 26/12/17.	
			79.42151 Pte. H. ALLEN Wounded 25/12/17.	
			" 27405 " A. WILLIAMS. D° 27/12/17.	
	9th		Draft of 13 O.R. arrived & posted to Coys.	
			Maj. W.H.G. GOATER M.C. returned from leave & assumed duties as 2nd in C.	
	10th		Draft of 2 O.R. arrived – posted to Coys.	
	11th		The F.M. C. in – C. renders authority granted by H.M. The King	
			awarded decorations as follows.	
			The Military Cross.	
			2nd Lt. F.D. SMITH	
			The Distinguished Conduct Medal	
			N° 235154 Sergt. J.W. THOMPSON	
			29265 Cpl. B. BUCKLEY.	

Army Form C. 2118.

WAR DIARY
or
INTELLIGENCE SUMMARY.
(Erase heading not required.)

Instructions regarding War Diaries and Intelligence Summaries are contained in F. S. Regs., Part II. and the Staff Manual respectively. Title pages will be prepared in manuscript.

Place	Date	Hour	Summary of Events and Information	Remarks and references to Appendices
FIELD	12th	17th	N-17937 PTE STARKES. KILLED. Following casualties from Hipptown be hand Gas 11/29/12/17. Mobilized in field hosp Wigonti- Capt. & Acy. A. Read N° 147731 SERJT DYSON G. " 19549 SERJT FOSTER E. " 19209 SERJT JACKSON G. N° 53215 RTE CAREY. D.W. WOUNDED 15/11/17 Capt. & Adjt. H. BASS returned from leave & resumed duties as Adjutant. MAJ. W.H.C. BEATER. M.C. took over command of Bn vice Lt.Col. R. HOWLETT D.S.O. M.C. to Brigade. Undermentioned Officers report of for duty:- 2nd Lt. H.W. McCARTHY 12/1/18 Lt. & QM. A. HUXLEY. 16/11/15. 2nd Lt. H. HALLS relinquished appointment as P.M.	

Army Form C. 2118.

WAR DIARY
or
INTELLIGENCE SUMMARY.
(Erase heading not required.)

N° 5

Place	Date	Hour	Summary of Events and Information	Remarks and references to Appendices
FIELD	22nd		CAPT. S.R. DOBINSON returned from leave - assumes command of B. Coy.	
	26.		2nd LT. W.H. ALLIS takes on duties as L.E.O. vice 2nd LT R. REDMOND. Draft of 37 O.R. reported & posted to Coys.	
	27th		LT. COL. F. HOWLETT D.S.O. resumed command of Bn. MAJ. W.H.C. BOATER A/Colonel retires vice 2nd in C. CAPT. J.R. STORT returned from leave & resumes command of "H" Coy vice LT. C. DAVISON. 2nd LT. J.E. HIRBERT reports & taken on strength & post to D. Coy.	

Epenall ells
Cdg 10 Yorkshire Regt

SECRET

10th Yorkshire Regiment
Order No. 15

1. 10th York R will relieve 12/13 NORTHUMBERLAND FUSILIERS in
left sub sector on night 12/13 January 1918 as follows & in following
order arriving at Bn HQ at times stated.

C Coy 10th YORK R will relieve	C Coy 12/13 N.F.	5·30 pm	R FRONT
A	A	5·45 pm	L
B	B	6·0 pm	RESERVE
D	D	6·15 pm	SUPPORT

   Times are subject to alteration.
   Relief complete will be notified by code word TOKE

2. Guides will not be required
   Advance parties consisting of 1 Officer 2 NCOs for front line Coys &
   HQ 2 NCOs for Support Coys will take over dispositions stores &c
   & will report to 12/13 N.F. HQ as follows:-
   LEFT FRONT 6am   BCD Coys & HQ at 2·30 pm

3. Gum boots will be taken over by one NCO C Coy at store in
   support line at 4 pm. Gum boots will be changed by C Coy
   on arrival (Leather boots will be carried up) to front line in
   sandbags).
   Gum boots for A Coy will be carried up by Transport

4. Blankets & packs will be dumped at R Coys HQ in hut by
   10 am. Transport Officer will arrange to move same to VILLERS
   FAUCON
   Spare kits, mess baskets & cooking utensils will be collected at
   4·30 pm
   Baskets to return by transport lines
   Water cart will supply water under same arrangements as last
   time in line
   Cooking arrangements as before

   K A James 2/Lieut Actg Adjt
                10 York R

11·1·18.

10th Bn Yorkshire Regt.   Office Copy
           Order No 45

SECRET
MAP REFERENCE
SIG. 2C
1/20000

The 10th Bn Yorks R. will relieve 12th & 13th NORTHUMBERLAND FUSILIERS in right &
left sub-sectors on the left sub-sector on [...] in following order:-

1. Relief will be interior by code word "READY".

   D Coy 10th YORK R.   by "D" Coy 14th NF   RIGHT FRONT
   B Coy   B Coy   LEFT
   A Coy   A Coy   COUNTER-ATTACKING COY
   C Coy   C Coy   SUPPORT COY

2. First Coys will pass Bn. Headqrs. at 5.30pm.
   "Quick will not" to signal.

3. Advance Parties   1 Officer per Coy & 1 N.C.O. per platoon will report
   to H.Q. 13th LINCOLNSHIRE REGIMENT by 2pm, to recce & take over.
   Advance Party for B Coy will go direct to PEZIERES.

4. On Relief B Coy will move to Sunken Road, PEZIERES W.30.a.9.2.
   A & D Coys & Headquarters to RAILWAY EMBANKMENT W.21.b.

5. Kit   Mens Blankets, Trench Kits & Cooking utensils will be dumped
   at Bn. Headqrs. by 5pm.   Transport Officer will arrange necessary
   transport for same.

   Lewis Guns.   Lewis Guns will be dumped by Coys. on the way out
   at Bn. Headqrs. & Transport Officer will arrange necessary transport
   to new positions.

   One Lewis Gun Section per Coy will remain at dump with guns Lewis
   gun & accompany Limbers to new positions.
   Sergt SOPP will take charge of dump.

6. Gum Boots   There will be no Gum Boots at the new positions. O.C. Coys
   will draw one Sandbag per man in which to carry down ankle boots.

7. Trench Stores   Lists of Trench Stores handed over will be forwarded
   to Bn. Headqrs. by 12 noon on 17th inst.

8. Blankets   Quartermaster will arrange to send up 1 Blanket per
   man to new positions.

9. Cookers   Transport Officer will arrange for 3 Cookers to be sent
   to RAILWAY EMBANKMENT.
   B Coy will cook in dixies at PEZIERES.

10. Dry Socks etc.   On arrival in new positions O C Coys will ensure
    that every man rubs his feet with whale oil & puts on a dry pair of
    socks.

                              R E James
                                      Lt & Acting Adjutant
                                      10th R. Yorkshire Regt.

January 16th 1918.

SECRET.

Map Ref. 57c. S.W. 1/20000.   Copy. No.

10th YORKSHIRE REGIMENT.
Order. No. 16.

1. 10th York. R. will relieve 12/13th NORTHD. FUS. on the night
20/21 inst. in the left sub-sector in the following order as
follows:-
   "A" Coy. 10.York.R. will relieve "A" Coy. 12/13. N.F.   LEFT FRONT.
   "C" Coy.   "   "   "   "C" Coy. "   "   RIGHT FRONT
   "B" Coy.   "   "   "   "B" Coy. "   "   Counterattack.Cy.
   "D" Coy.   "   "   "   "D" Coy. "   "   Support Coy.
Companies will pass Headquarters 12/13 N.F. at the following times:-
   "C" Coy. 8-30p.m. "A" Coy. 8-45p.m. "B" Coy. 9-00p.m.
   "D" Coy. 9-0.p.m. Bn. H.Q. 9-15p.m.
Relief complete will be notified by wiring the word "HUBERT"

2. Guides will not be provided.

3. An advance party consisting of Lieut A.B. Griffin and the R.S.M.
reach 13th N.F. Hdqrs. at 5.P.M.

4. All Mess baskets and Trench Kits and Cooking Utensils of A.C.
& D. Coys. will be dumped at Bn. Hdqrs. at 8.p.m. The Transport
Officer will arrange necessary transport. Kits etc. of B. Coy will
be collected from B. Coy. Hdqrs. at 7:30 p.m.

5. Lewis Guns will be dumped by Coys. at Bn. Hdqrs. at 7-30p.m.
(B.Coy at Coy. Hdqrs.) The transport Officer will arrange transport
for same.
   One Lewis Gun Section per Coy. will remain with the Guns to load
same and accompany limbers. Sergt GADD will take charge of the
dump at present Bn. Hdqrs. The R.S.M. will take charge of the
dump at new Bn. Hdqrs. (This dump will be in the Sunken Road
at C.18-b, 80.30
   Lewis Gun Magazines will be taken over. One Lewis Gun N.C.O. per
Coy. will report at Bn. Hdqrs 12/13 N.F. at 3p.m. to take over
these Magazines.

6. Gum Boots. Gum Boots will be worn by men going up. O.C. Coys.
will draw one sand bag per man at 12 noon to-morrow from Bn. Hdqrs which
will be used for carrying up ankle boots. These sandbags will be used
for repair of trenches.

7. Trench Stores. List of Trench stores taken over will be forwarded to
Bn. Hdqrs. by 12 noon on the 21st inst.

8. Blankets. O.C. Coys will arrange for blankets to be dumped at Coy.
Hdqrs. by 11 a.m. The T.O. will arrange to collect same at this time.

9. Socks. Socks will be changed daily whilst in the line. The Qmr. will
arrange for the necessary supply.

10. Returns. Usual returns will be rendered.

11. Acknowledge.

                                            Capt. & Adjt.
                                            10th York. R.

1-2-3. War Diary and File.   8. T.O.
4.   O.C. A. Coy.   9. Ord.
5.   O.C. C. Coy.   10. M.O.
6.   O.C. B. Coy.   11. Signal O.
7.   O.C. D. Coy.   12. H.Q.Mess.
                             13. R.S.M.
                             14. 62nd Inf. Bde (for Information)
                             15. 12/13. Northd. Fus.

10TH MACHINE SECTION
ADDENDA TO S.A.O. NO. 14.

Reference Para. 5.
Lewis Gun Magazines will not be handed over; they will be
taken in with the Guns. The I.S. N.C.O. will not report at
30,E.

Issued as per order No. 14.   [signature]
   19.1.18
                                      Capt. & Adjt.
                                      10th.York.Regt.

SECRET.
Map.Ref. 57c.S.E, 1/20000   Copy.No.2.

                        10.Yorkshire Regiment
                           Order No. 1M.

1. RELIEF.   "B" & "D" Coys . will relieve "A" & "C" Coy respectively
             in the front line to-night.
             Relief will commence as soon as working parties permit.
             i,e, about 10-30p,m.
             Relief complete will be reported by the Word "WELL".

2. GUM BOOTS. "B" & "D" Coys will change into dry boots before proceeding
             on working party , and will dump wet boots at Bn. Hdqrs.
             under R.S.M's instructions.
             Dry Boots will be drawn from same place.

3. FEET.   Whale oil will be used and dry socks put on by "B" & "D" Coys
             before relief.

4. WIRING.   O.C. "A" Coy will relieve the wiring party of "B" Coy.

5. ACKNOWLEDGE.

                                                        [signature]
                                                        Capt & Adjt.
                                                        10.Yorks. R.

1-2-3- War Diary & File.   9. Qr,Mr.
4. O.C. A. Coy.   10. M.O.
5.   B. Coy.   11. Signal,O.
6.   C. Coy.   12. Hdqr Mess.
7.   D. Coy.   13. R.S.M.
8.   T.O.   14. 62nd Inf. Bde. (for information)

SECRET.
Map Ref. 57.S.E. 1/20000.
Copy No. 1.....

10.YORKSHIRE REGIMENT&
Order No. 18.

1. **RELIEF.** 10.York Regt. will be relieved by 12/13th NORTHD FUS. on night of 24th January. 1918. in the left sub-sector as follows and in the following order:-
   Relief completed will be notified by the code word "CYRIL"
   "D" Coy. 10.York.R. by "D" Coy. 12/13.N.F.   Right Front.
   "B"   "   "   "B" Coy.   "   Left Front.
   "C" Coy.   "   "C" Coy.   "   Support Coy.
   "A" Coy.   "   "A" Coy.   "   Counter attacking Coy

   First Coy. passes Bn. H.Q. at 7-15p,m.
   On relief Bn. will move to HEUDECOURT and will become Brigade Reserve.

2. **GUIDES.** Guides will not be required.

3. **ADVANCE PARTY.** Lieut A.E. Griffin. R.S.M. 1 Officer per Coy and 1 N.C.O. per platoon will report to H.Q. 1st LINCOLN Regt. at HEUDECOURT at 2p,m, to take over.

4. **KIT.** Mess Baskets, Trench Kits, Cooking Utensils and O.R. Stores will be dumped at BN.H.Q. by 6-30p,m. The Transport Officer will arrange necessary transport for same.

5. **LEWIS GUNS.** Lewis Guns will be dumped by Coys on way out in the SUNKEN ROAD at W.18.b.80.30. Transport Officer to arrange necessary transport for same.
   1 L.G. Section per Coy.will remain at Dump to load same and accompany Limbers.
   1 Police detailed by R.S.M. to take charge of Dump.

6. **GUM BOOTS.** These will be worn by men going out. Where necessary O.C. Coys will draw from R.S.M. one sand bag per man to carry ankle boots.

7. **TRENCH STORES.** Lists of Stores handed over will be forwarded to Bn. H.Q. by 12 noon 25th inst.

8. **BLANKETS.** The Qr.Mr.will send up Two Blankets per man to HEUDECOURT.

9. **SOCKS.** On arrival at HEUDECOURT. O.C. Coys will ensure that every man rubs his feet with whale oil and puts on a dry pair of socks. Qr.Mr. to ensure supply of Whale Oil & Socks.

10. **ACKNOWLEDGE.**

                                                    Capt & Adjt.
                                                    10.York.Regt.

1-2-3- War Diary & File.   10. M.O.
4.   O.C. A. Coy.   11. S.O.
5.   B, Coy.   12. H.Q.Mess.
6.   C. Coy.   13. R.S.M.
7.   D, Coy.   14. 62nd Inf. Bde. For Information.
8.   T.O.   15. 12/13th Northd. Fus.
9.   Qr.Mr.

SECRET.   COPY No. 2

Map.Ref. 57c.S.E.1/20000.

10th YORKSHIRE REGIMENT.

Order No.19.

1. **RELIEF.** 10th Yor.R. Will relieve 12/13th Northumberland Fus. on the night of 28/29th Jan.1918 in the left sub-sector as follows:-

   "A" Coy. 10.York.R. will relieve "A" Coy. 12/13th.N.F. Left Front
   "C" Coy.   do   do   "C" Coy.   do   Right "
   "B" Coy.   "   "   "B" "   "   Counter attack-
                                                              ing Coy.
   "D" Coy.   "   "   "D" "   "   Supports.

   Companies will leave present camp at the following times:-
   C. Coy 4-50p.m, "A" Coy. 5 p.m. "B" Coy 5-10p.m,.
   "D" Coy. 5-20p.m. Hdqrs 5-30p.m.
   Relief complete will be notified by wiring the code word "VIVIAN"

2. **GUIDES.** Guides will not be provided.

3. **ADVANCE PARTY.** An advance party consisting of Lieut A.E. Griffin and R.S.M. will reach H.Q. 12/13th N.F. at 3p.m.

4. **TRENCH KITS.** All Mess Baskets, Trench Kits and Cooking Utensils and O.R. Stores will be dumped near "B" Coy. Orderly Room by 5 p.m. Transport Officer will arrange necessary Transport.

5. **LEWIS GUNS.** Lewis Guns will be dumped by Coys. near "B" Coy. O.R. by 4 p.m. The Transport Officer will arrange transport for same. One Lewis Gun section per company will remain with the Guns to load same and will accompany the limbers. Sergt CADD will take charge of this Dump.

6. **GUM BOOTS.** Unless the weather is bad Gum Boots will not be taken

7. **BLANKETS. ETC.** O.C. Companies will arrange for Blankets to be dumped at Company Headquarters at 11 a.m. Officers Kits will be dumped at Hdqrs and Company H.Q. at 3 p.m. The Transport Officer will arrange necessary Transport. Orderly Room Stores (less Typewriter) will be taken to transport lines.

8. **SOCKS.** Socks will be changed daily while in the line. The Qr.Mr will arrange necessary supply.

9. **RETURNS.** The usual returns will be rendered. Receipted copies of Trench stores will be forwarded to Bn. H.Q, by 12 noon on the 29th inst.

10. **ACKNOWLEDGE.**

                                           H.Bas., Capt & Adjt.
                                                   10.YORK.R.

1-2-3- War Diary & File.
4.   O.C. A. Coy.
5,   B. Coy.
6.   C. Coy.
7.   D. Coy.
8.   T.O.
9.   Qr.Mr.
10.   M.O.
11.   S.O.
12.   Hdqr.Mess.
13.   R.S.M.
14.   62nd Inf. Bde. (for information)
15.   12/13th North. Fus.

Copy No. 2
Jan. 29th 1918.

10th Yorkshire Regiment.
OPERATION ORDER

1. **RELIEF.** 137th Inf. Bde. will relieve 62nd Inf. Bde. on the left sector of the Divisional front on January 30th 1918.
   10th Rifle Bde. will relieve 10th Yorks. in the Left Sub-sector.

2. **GUIDES.** a. One Guide per Company will report to the Adjutant at C-4?a,?, 30-1-18. These Guides will meet the incoming Bn. at Bde. Hdqrs and bring them to present Bn. Hdqrs.
   b. 1 Guide per post and 1 for Coy. H.Q. will report to Bn. H.Q. at C-30c,?. These Guides will take incoming Companies direct to their posts.
   (a) Guides will be provided with a slip stating Company, O.C. Right Front Line Coy.
   (b) Guides will be provided with notes stating exactly which posts they are for.

3. **DOCUMENTS.** Programmes of Work, Defence Schemes, Maps, Aeroplane Photographs, Grenades, R.O.P. Signals, etc. and all documents relating to the sector will be handed over on relief.

4. **Trench STORES.** Lists of Trench Stores to be handed over will be forwarded to Bn. H.Q. by 12 noon 30th inst. Receipted lists will be forwarded as early as possible after arrival in new area.

5. **BLANKETS.** All Officers Kits, Mess Baskets and Cooking Utensils will be on the St. Dump by 6 a.m. The Transport Officer will arrange to collect these at this time.
   Time for Lewis Gun Limbers will be notified later.

6. **ENTRAINING.** Details with regard to entraining will be issued later.

7. Relief complete will be notified to Bn. H.Q. by Code word "ARTHUR".

8. **TRANSPORT.** The Transport Officer will make his own arrangements for the Transport to proceed to ETRELAINES.

9. **BILLETS.** The Qr. Mr. with billeting party from the stores will arrange to meet the Battalion at detraining station, and will arrange billets for the Bn.

10. **BUGLE PARTY.** Bugle Party now at Transport Lines will march under the Senior Officer to the new area, under arrangements made by Senior Officer.

H. Bass
Capt & Adjt.
10. YORK R.

Distribution.
1-2-3- War Diary & File.   8. T.O.
4.   O.C. A. Coy.   9. Qr. Mr.   14. 62nd Inf. Bde (for
5.   B. Coy.   10. M.O.   Information)
6.   C. Coy.   11. S.O.   15. 10th Rifle Bde.
7.   D. Coy.   12. H.Q. Mess.
                               13. R.S.M.

www.ingramcontent.com/pod-product-compliance
Lightning Source LLC
Chambersburg PA
CBHW080907230426
43664CB00016B/2749